| AUTHOR | CLASS |
|---|---|
| SHEPLEY, A. | C051 |

**TITLE**

Lancashire: walks for motorists

# LANCASHIRE
## WALKS FOR MOTORISTS

*Countryside Books' walking guides cover most areas of England and Wales and include the following series:*

*County Rambles*
*Walks For Motorists*
*Exploring Long Distance Paths*
*Literary Walks*
*Pub Walks*

*A complete list is available from the publishers.*

# LANCASHIRE

## WALKS FOR MOTORISTS

Alan Shepley

30 Walks with sketch maps

COUNTRYSIDE BOOKS
NEWBURY, BERKSHIRE

First published 1993
© Alan Shepley 1993

COUNTRYSIDE BOOKS
3 Catherine Road
Newbury, Berkshire

ISBN 1 85306 214 6

05765551

Cover photograph of Rossendale Green
taken by the author

**Publishers' Note**
At the time of publication all rights of way were shown on the definitive
maps maintained by local councils or were well-established permitted
routes, but it should be borne in mind that diversion orders may be made
from time to time and permissions may be withdrawn.

Produced through MRM Associates Ltd., Reading
Typeset by Paragon Typesetters, Queensferry, Clwyd
Printed in England by J. W. Arrowsmith Ltd., Bristol

# Contents

# Key to Sketch Maps

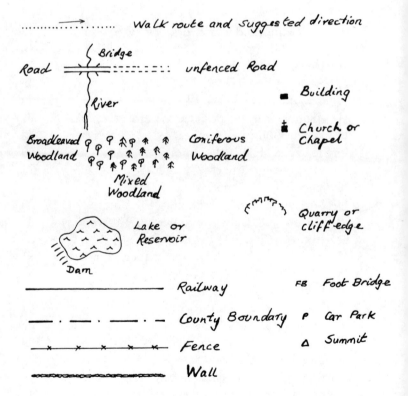

........→........ Walk route and suggested direction

Road ═══╪═══ :···········: unfenced Road
        Bridge

        River                          ■ Building

                                       ⛪ Church or
                                          Chapel

Broadleaved ♀ ♀ ♀ ⋔ ♀ ⋔   Coniferous
Woodland    ♀ ♀ ♀ ⋔ ⋔ ⋔   Woodland
            ♀ ♀ ⋔ ♀ ⋔ ♀ ⋔ ⋔
                Mixed
                Woodland                  Quarry or
                                          cliff edge

            Lake or
            Reservoir

        Dam

——————————— Railway              FB  Foot Bridge

—— · —— · —— · — County Boundary   P  Car Park

—×——×——×——×——× Fence              △  Summit

~~~~~~~~~~~~~~~ Wall

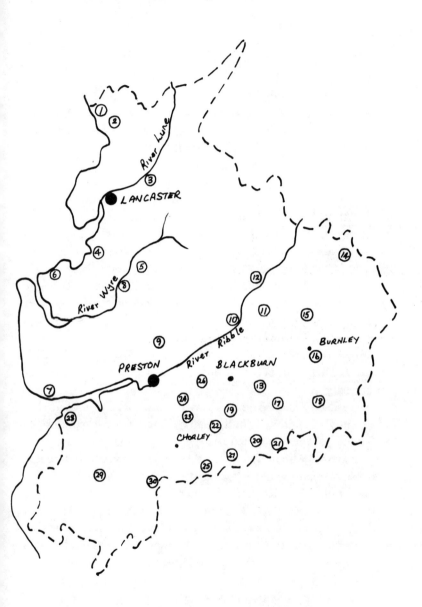

Area map showing location of the walks.

# Introduction

Choosing just 30 walks to include has proved extremely difficult. The countryside of the county of Lancashire is so varied in its nature that the potential for walking, even by the modest criteria of avoiding the more difficult ground, keeping entirely on public rights of way or well-established permitted routes, and not being too ambitious in length, gives a lifetime or two of opportunity. In the final analysis I have opted to ensure there is a walk within each and every district and to choose, as far as is practicable, walks which offer the added pleasure of observing wildlife, delving into our historical past, or enjoying some other aspect of the present as well as the walk itself.

The walks vary in length from 2½ to 8¾ miles but the time you need to devote to each is very dependent on the weather and your interest in the other possibilities referred to, like museums and nature reserves, as well as on your own speed of walking. There is, I trust, a sufficient choice to allow you to stride out if you wish on occasion or to wander, gently, with plenty to see as you go.

Accessibility to our rights of way has improved immeasurably in recent years and most of the paths are clearly marked by signs where they leave a metalled road, or by the now familiar stubby yellow arrows which often point the way in between. Where this was not the case when I last used each route the combination of sketch map and description should enable you to find the way without difficulty. The Ordnance Survey Landranger 1:50 000 scale map sheet numbers are given for each walk and carrying the appropriate map with you should resolve any residual doubts on the ground. Do remember, nonetheless, that the countryside is never static and changes in routes (usually minor, let it be said) are continually taking place. Local advice is always worth listening to.

Whether it is derived from coal-measure sandstone and shale, limestone, or from the lower-lying glacial deposits, the soil of Lancashire is liable to be clarty from time to time. Except perhaps for one exception, these walks do require reasonable footwear – though they do not need heavy boots. The very juxtaposition of sea, plain, and the hills results in ever-changing patterns of weather so it is unwise indeed to move off without protection from rain in all but the most settled spells of high pressure.

I am greatly indebted to many good friends who have walked these ways with me over many years and to those who have, before me, written so enticingly of walking in Lancashire and of the history and natural history of the county. The literature of walking is like that of gardening and cookery – always the same at first sight and always different in its detail and its outcomes. If this further addition to it brings but one individual or family to a greater joy in, and awareness of, the variety of Lancashire I shall be well pleased. Whilst enjoying it we should also all respect it and remember that there are, often hard, livings being made in the countryside; please do follow the Country Code:

Enjoy the countryside and respect its life and work
Guard against all risk of fire
Fasten all gates
Keep your dogs under close control
Keep to public paths across farmland
Use gates and stiles to cross fences, hedges and walls
Leave livestock, crops and machinery alone
Take your litter home
Help to keep all water clean
Protect wildlife, plants and trees
Take special care on country roads
Make no unnecessary noise

Alan Shepley
March 1993

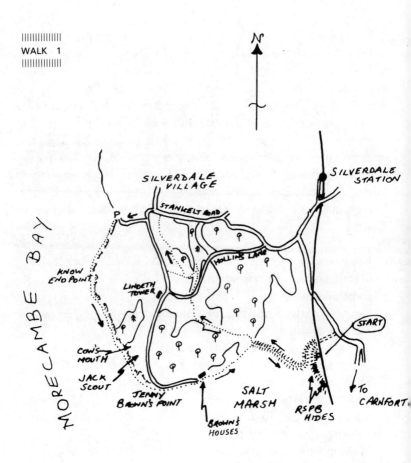

N

MORECAMBE BAY

SILVERDALE
VILLAGE

SILVERDALE
STATION

STANWELT ROAD

P

HOLLINS LANE

KNOW
END POINT

LINDETH
TOWER

START

COW'S
MOUTH

JACK
SCOUT

JENNY
BROWN'S POINT

SALT
MARSH

TO
CARNFORT

BROWN'S
HOUSES

RSPB
HIDES

# SILVERDALE SHORE

## WALK 1

★

4 miles (6.5 km)

OS Landranger 97

The shimmering sea of Morecambe Bay and the rocks around are as silver now as when a Norseman called Soelvers gave his name to this place about the year AD900. A thousand years of tide and storm have moulded the bay and cliffs and man has left his mark on the woods, fields and shore as well as on the village itself. Before the railway came in the 1850s the mosses made Silverdale relatively inaccessible. Once travel was easy, many south Lancashire industrialists made their retirement and holiday homes here and it is still a popular place to retire to.

The best approach is from the A6 at Carnforth. Just past Crag Foot turn along the track beside the Silverdale sign and under the railway arch to use the car park for the RSPB public hides from which the birds of the saltmarsh can be viewed (GR: SD 475736).

Cross the bridge seaward of the railway and on to the embankment. If you look below the bridge you can see the sluices which control the water flow off Leighton Moss (an RSPB reserve) and back at Crag Foot the chimney of the old pumping station still stands as a memorial to efforts at drainage which ended in 1917.

Walk round the embankment with fine views out across the marsh and evidence of winter storms in the flotsam caught in the fence. At the path junction follow the sign marked 'Woodwell' through the iron gate and left uphill beside the wall to a thorn tree literally growing out of a boulder. Warton Crag dominates the view across the valley and the RSPB hides are visible on the embankment.

A stile leads to an open area where you bear a little right by the wire fence to another stile and follow the left hand wall over the brow. Here there is a superb view of Arnside Knott and the Lakeland fells. Keep round the back of the barn and on to a track which leads to Hollins Lane. Cross the lane to pick up the signed path again; go right through the wood and above a cliff with massive detached blocks separated from it. You will see the collecting basin of Woodwell below. A path goes diagonally down the cliff about 50 yards beyond and leads to the stone trough under an overhang into which water unfailingly drips. This is the largest of several wells in Silverdale which seem to be fed in artesian fashion from reservoirs in the rock below, so making habitation of this limestone area practicable.

Follow the sign 'To the Village', turn right opposite 'Ivyleigh' through a stile and continue, along the backs of gardens with woods on your right, past a small white cottage to emerge close to the village centre. The off licence doubles as an information centre and several shops, hostelries, and a tea shop are to hand. Just beyond is the Gaskell Memorial Hall, named after the writer of 'Cranford' who spent many summers at Lindeth Tower in the 1850s.

Retrace your steps to the road junction and turn down towards the shore. Lindeth Road bears left to Lindeth Tower and the Wolf House Gallery, built in 1790. An older house dated 1749 is almost opposite the Silverdale Hotel.

At the shore itself is a car park which is liable to flooding by the tide. This is a good place to stop, admire the view across to Humphrey Head and Grange-over-Sands, and to take stock. On a December day of brilliant light I sat in warm sun on the rocks here and lunched on a locally bought pasty watching shelduck and redshank. Should the tide be coming in it would be wise to return to Lindeth Road and walk through to the Point since it would be dangerous to use the shore itself.

The saltmarsh has been eroded and has gone entirely from the base of the shattered limestone of the cliffs for much of the way round the Point. As a consequence you will find yourself using the sand on occasions. Be cautious here for, just as the main bay is notorious for quicksands which yearly claim the lives of the unwary, even the sand close inshore can be very soft and the chance for a quick step back on to solid rock gives confidence.

In places paths can be seen reaching the cliff top and you should not hesitate to use them if need be. At the end of most of them a Parish Council notice warns of the quicksands and the speed of the incoming tide. The Queen's Guide to the Bay, Cedric Robinson, lives at Kents Bank near Grange-over-Sands (Guides Farm, Cart Lane. Tel: 05395 32165) and will guide you safely across the sands for a fee; these days it is a popular way of raising funds for charity.

Beyond Know End Point a fresh water spring bubbles out at the foot of the cliff and the thorn trees at its top are bent double by the sea wind. The obvious cove is Cow's Mouth where cattle may perhaps have come ashore after passage across the sands on their way to market. On the far side is a short exploratory mine adit which shows the drill holes for the blasting powder in its walls. The knoll above is a National Trust property called Jack Scout and is crowned by a stone seat and the remains of a lime kiln. The farthest reach of the headland is Jenny Brown's Point. Here the remains of the last embankment attempting to enclose land from the bay stretch forlornly out seaward. The voice of money won the parliamentary day in 1875 despite much local opposition but the bay began to reclaim its own a mere ten years later.

Shortly, join a path which meets the road running down to Brown's Houses by the shore. Just beyond stands the chimney of a copper works which operated during the Napoleonic Wars. The ore was mined from the limestone locally – perhaps the adit at Cow's Mouth was an attempt to find more. Continue along the marsh edge (taking care with an extremely wobbly stile) to join your initial route at the end of the embankment. Return along this to the start.

# WARTON CRAG

## WALK 2

★

2 ¾  miles (4.5 km)

OS Landranger 97

Warton Crag is the limestone hill (535 ft) behind Warton village, which is so clearly seen from the M6 to the west of Junction 35. Most of it is a designated Site of Special Scientific Interest, and there is access at all times on permitted paths to adjoining nature reserves; one is operated jointly by Lancashire Trust for Nature Conservation and Lancaster City Council, and the other by the Royal Society for the Protection of Birds. The latter has a dedication to Mary Goodheart – recorded on a polished black granite block let in to the limestone wall on Crag Road.

Start by following the many signs to the village centre and then the English Heritage sign for the car park in the old quarry on Crag Road a few yards from The Black Bull pub (GR: SD 498724). The route is an asymmetrical figure of eight with a tail to the Steamtown Railway Museum at Carnforth. I suggest starting with the Crag itself.

Take the stony path at the top of the car park to a gap in the wall with a nature reserve sign and map just beyond; fossil corals and sea-lilies are exposed in the quarry face. Turn right a few paces and then left to walk gradually up among a series of small limestone cliffs. Some care is needed here, especially when the rock is wet, and children should be well watched. The turf on these limestone ledges is particularly rich in flowers and has a glorious sequence of species and white, yellow, blue, and red flowers from early spring through to September. It is also a place in which many of the rarer plants are very sensitive to trampling and you should try not to walk on the turf itself. In several areas

15

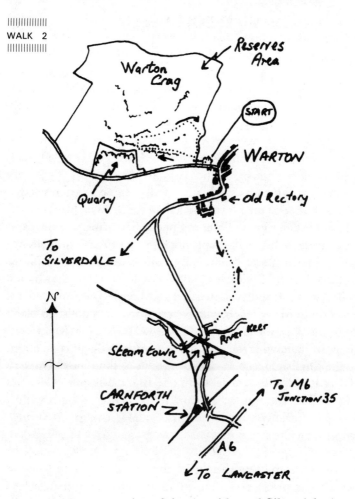

the management service of the Arnside and Silverdale Area of Outstanding Natural Beauty has been carrying out work to protect the rarer species and increase the variety of plants and animals.

All the way along at the foot of the cliff are screes of broken limestone, mostly a result of the last Ice Age but still being added to by the erosive effects of winter weather. Many of the trees are dark-foliaged yews, and the deep-pink flowered garden escapee Red Valerian has taken hold here.

16

The path eventually reaches the boundary wall of the RSPB reserve at a stile above a large quarry. The view from here is wide and takes in Pine Lodge Resort, in the old gravel pits to the east beside the M6, Warton just below, Carnforth across the River Keer, the wide sands of Morecambe Bay with Heysham Nuclear Power Station standing out on the far shore, and Blackpool Tower way beyond. Round the Crag to your right close to Crag Foot, caves have yielded Stone Age and Romano-British artefacts which are now on display in Lancaster Museum and immediately above, on the crest, are the remains of a British hill-fort of Roman date.

Turn up the hill on to a more substantial terrace where deeper soil has accumulated and bracken and blackthorn thickets grow. In this scrub area yellowhammers and whitethroats are common. Turn right again and follow the path to come to an extensive area of limestone pavement on your left in about 300 yards. Erosion by rain and frost has caused the vertical joints to be opened out into grykes, leaving worn blocks, or clints, between. Within the grykes it is very sheltered and a variety of trees have taken root in some areas – juniper, holly, oak, ash, and hazel, amongst others. The path continues on to the boundary wall. Bear right and downwards to return to the sign and the point at which you entered the reserve.

Back at the car park, walk down the hill to the pub and turn right past the village hall to the 14th century church of St Oswald. Immediately inside the door to the left is a family tree of the Washington family (ancestors of George Washington) and at several other places more information is on display. A carved stone let in to the wall of the vestry under the tower shows the coat of arms from which the Stars and Stripes may be derived.

Almost immediately across the road from the church is the entrance to Warton Old Rectory (English Heritage), open each day (except Mondays between October and Easter, and Christmas and New Year's Day). This is the ruin of a 14th century manor house, the oldest in the county, and well worth at least a brief visit even for those uninterested in the fine detail of mediaeval architecture.

Rather than end the walk at this point you can add the short ¾ mile via the footpath at the end of Gardner Road (signed to Millhead) to Steamtown, on the Warton road at the edge of Carnforth. Anyone with a hint of the romance of the railways in their soul, or children of any age to amuse, will find here one of the finest museums in the country. The collection, on the engine shed site last used by British Rail in 1968, includes freight as well as passenger locomotives and is open from April to the end of December. You will need to check which are full and which minor operating days (Tel: 0524 734220). There is also a mile of operational narrow gauge track, a model railway, a museum, a shop and a buffet.

# CASTLES IN
# THE VALE OF LUNE

## WALK 3

★

7½ miles (12 km)

OS Landranger 97

The number of fortified sites along the Vale of Lune comes as a considerable surprise in this day and age, when the valley has all the appearance of always having been a quiet rural backwater. The Romans had been here first, of course, at Burrow and Lancaster itself. But it was the Norman Conquest, following upon the Scandinavian settlements of perhaps 150 years before, which led to a reorganisation of the area into a borderland, the remains of which are still identifiable. Before 1066, much of this country was in the hands of Earl Tostig of Northumbria, the brother of King Harold who fought against him at Stamford Bridge. For almost 30 years after that the border between England and Scotland was unsettled and Cumbria north and west of the Lakeland fells was Scots which meant that the estates held by Roger of Poitou, and based on Lancaster, were in the first line of defence. Only when William Rufus took Carlisle in 1092 did the line move forward and even then the whole area between the Lune and the Solway remained an intermittent battleground for another 400 years. This figure-of-eight walk takes a look at some of the surviving evidence of these and ensuing centuries.

The best place to start is at the crossing of the Lune at the old Loyn Bridge on the lane to Gressingham just north of Hornby village on the A683, the Lancaster to Kirkby Lonsdale road. Park on the Gressingham side of the river (GR: SD 580697).

Take the signed path upstream; half right the view is out onto Caton Moor and Goodber Common. Willows and alders on the

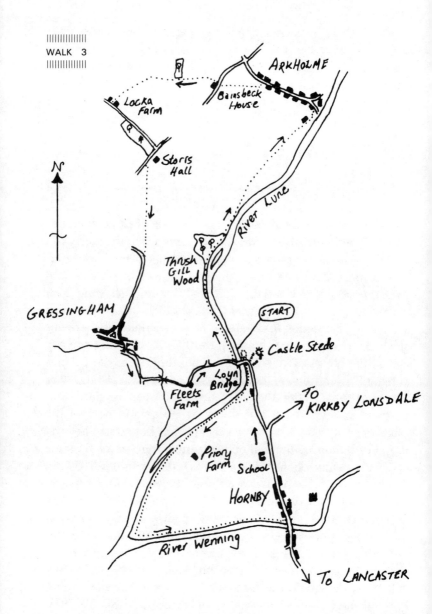

bank always have flood debris caught high in their branches and the ever-changing shape of the shingle banks indicates the winter force of the river. Thrush Gill Wood has much sycamore and beech, and the occasional lime, and tends to be rather wet underfoot. Fish jump in the deeper pools here and there are usually mallard dabbling. At the far end of the wood a footbridge leads out into fields and the path stays down close to the river and goes towards, and right of, a white cottage. Here there used to be a ford across the river from the Scandinavian-named Arkholme up on the bank on your left. Unless the river is caught at very low water it is impracticable now though a footpath still leads to either side of it. On the river bank here, in winter, large flocks of Canada geese gather. Out, across the river, the interesting church of Melling, with its Scandinavian-style cross, is in sight. In the trees behind it lies the mound of a motte and bailey castle.

Much closer, as you turn left along the lane up the bank and into the village of Arkholme, is the motte of another castle. On top of it stands the church of St John the Baptist. This has a bell dated at the turn of the 14th century but the bellcote and pediment is about 1700 and the rest a rebuilding of 1897. Looking up river from the churchyard you can see the bridge of the Skipton-Carnforth railway line.

Turn away from the river now and along the pretty village street of stone houses and garden walls covered in ivy-leaved toadflax. Just beyond Poole House (dated 1614) go left at the gate and bear right after the stile, following the arrow through gates and aim for the left hand of a row of four yew trees to exit onto a lane opposite Bainsbeck House. Turn right and then cross the lane to go up the track at the right of the farm buildings. Head across the field to the left of a small wood and continue to a footbridge to the left by a post. Climb up the brow a short way to the farmhouse of Locka and turn left at the lane. Walk along past Locka Wood of pine and beech on your right, with wide views up the Vale of Lune and the mounded landscape of glacial drumlins, to a T junction. Across the lane is the imitation Tudor Gothic mansion of Storrs Hall. Built by a Kirkby Lonsdale solicitor in 1848 on the site of an earlier house, it even has an imitation defensive pele tower.

Walk right, past the main gates, and cross to a green gate

in the wall and onto a path signed to Gressingham. At the field go half right and go ahead over the fields with Hornby castle in view down the valley on the other side of the river. Exit onto a lane at a right-angled bend and turn left down into Gressingham village and bear left to St John's church on the corner of a lane signed to Eastrigge. The original church is Norman, as the doorway shows, but was extensively rebuilt in 1734. Inside is the elaborate tomb of George Marton, MP for Lancaster from 1837.

Drop down to cross Gressingham Beck over a stone bridge and bear left and left again past the cottages. As you go down towards Fleet Bridge the view is of the beech and pine plantations beyond Hornby and the high hedges and banks provide shelter for a host of wild flowers in the verges. At the Gressingham lane turn right and over Loyn Bridge. For the moment, resist the temptation to look at Castle Stede but, instead, assuming the river is low enough, turn to the left through an iron gate and come round under the bridge to pick up the rather indistinct path through the wood along the river bank in a down-stream direction. (If the water is high there is the alternative of going up the lane above the wood and turning right on the path beyond the bungalow of Lune Cottage.) The path leads now along the river bank to the confluence with the river Wenning and then turns back up to the bridge in Hornby village. These are obviously wide flats formed by flooding and are mostly one huge field where curlew and oystercatcher cry overhead. Along the way you pass behind Priory Farm on the bank above; this was once a daughter house of the Premonstratensian Abbey of Croxton in Leicestershire. At the point where the rivers join the view straight ahead to the hamlet of Farleton includes the site of yet another castle, none of which is now left standing.

The walk up by the Wenning into Hornby is dominated by the impressive pile of Hornby castle, despite some modern houses on the edge of the village. At the main road it is worth walking up onto the far side of the bridge to get the best, and very picturesque, view. What you see is a considerable 19th century extension built on to a 13th century pele tower which had already been altered in the 16th century. Sometime in the early 1100s Hornby became the seat of the lordship of Montbegon, for many years equal in status to Lancaster. The original castle seems to have been that at Castle Stede and the centre of activity only moved to Hornby when the Nevilles succeeded to the lordship in the 13th century. Later the lordship passed to a scion of the Earls of Derby, Lord Mounteagle, who had led the men of Lancashire on Flodden Field. It was he who had the church of St Margaret built in 1514 with its unusual two-stage octagonal tower, with a half twist between the two stages. The east end has an equally rare polygonal shape and there is a tablet (in a C of E church) to the Roman Catholic priest-historian, Dr Lingard, dated 1851, whose own church of St Mary lies a little to the east across the street.

Continue through the village and past the secondary school to turn left down the lane towards Gressingham. This is lined with some fine sycamores on the right. Beyond Lune Cottage there is a footpath on the right which goes almost immediately past the entrance of Castle Stede. This is one of the finest motte and bailey castles remaining in England – and the reason for saving it until last. The site is private and permission to enter and view the whole site should be requested. As you return to the lane and go down to the bridge it is worth glancing at the side of the mound where the river cobbles used to strengthen it have been exposed by erosion.

# GLASSON AND THURNHAM

WALK 4

★

4½ miles (7 km)

OS Landranger 102

This is a fine walk for all seasons and all tastes with easy going and well within the scope of an active family. It combines natural history, industrial archaeology, history and a varied scene so you should expect to be happily waylaid for hours by matters of interest at several places as well as finding a choice of refreshment.

Approach the start by using the A588 either from the south end of Lancaster city or via the B5272 from Garstang to Cockerham. At Conder Green, just north of the B5290 turn for Glasson, take the unfenced track by The Stork inn to the car park of the picnic site at the former station overlooking the saltmarshes of the mouth of the River Lune (GR: SD 457561); there are toilets here.

Join the old railway track at the sign for the Lancashire Coastal Way by the entrance to the car park and walk along the railway bed over the bridge across the river Conder. The long view across the tidal marshes is rather dominated these days by Heysham Nuclear Power Station but the foreground of boats, fishermen and bird life gives an instant sense of timelessness. All the way along to Glasson there is opportunity to bird-watch to your heart's content. On a bright, February day I found no difficulty in clocking up herring, lesser black-backed, and black-headed gulls, curlew, lapwing, knot, shelduck, redshank, wigeon, coot, heron and crow – and there were, no doubt, other waders present I am not skilful enough to distinguish without book or

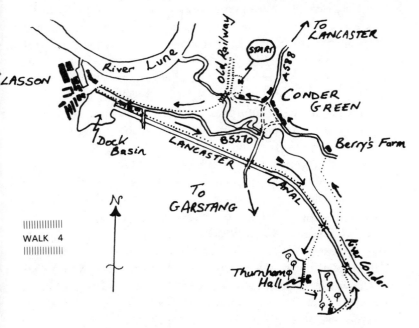

WALK 4

expert to hand. Once the surfaced path is ended and you have reached the road, stay on the grass as far as the bowling green and toilets by the Victoria Inn – the first building on this side.

Glasson is a mini-mecca for trippers in the summer and offers a burger-bar and restaurant on a boat in the dock basin at that season. At all times there are three pubs, a couple of other cafés, and a shop and post office on Tithebarn Hill. An information board and map are provided on the dockside.

The dock was built at Glasson around 1750 to overcome the silting up of the port of Lancaster itself. In 1826 a short branch of the Lancaster Canal was built from just south of Galgate to link Glasson with Kendal to the north, Preston to the south, and with centres further afield. Competition from Fleetwood, Heysham, Barrow and, of course, Liverpool and Manchester, slowly drew trade away from Lancaster and the railway, built in 1887 by the London & North Western Railway Company (the 'Little' North Western), was a last attempt to defeat the inevitable; passenger services ended in 1930, a daily goods train ran until just after World War II and the line was finally closed in 1964. Glasson is, however, by no means dead as a port though it mostly accommodates pleasure craft now. A few merchant craft dock from time to time. Some, like the *Bjarköy* out of Tromsö in arctic Norway, are surprisingly exotic, and you may well see the local fishery protection vessel *L & W Protector*.

Walk back along the upper, and larger, dock basin. At the landward end is a pleasant picnic site and an opportunity to sit and watch the boats or the ducks, swans, and gulls in the dock. A cast-iron signpost points to the 'Canal Main Line' along the towpath; take this route inland now. A few steps along on the left is the pleasant red sandstone Christ Church of 1840 with its bellcote and graveyard by the canal side. Away towards the hills, Lancaster University is in view on Bailrigg and, behind the city itself, the domed Ashton Memorial in Williamson Park. The first stone bridge is No.8 and the grassy towpath here becomes muddy after rain. The reed-grass provides cover in the canal edge for nesting coot and moorhen and nods its feathery seed-heads in the breeze. By the next bridge you are out amongst sheep-grazed fields and at No.6 go beneath the main road and shortly come to the first lock beside Thurnham Mill, now a pub and restaurant. Those who need to shorten their walk can cut back to Conder Green from here.

Pass a second lock and, at the next bridge go up and cross over to the other side of the canal. Bear half left to a stile by a gate and follow an old track, between high hedges at first, and then across a field to the right of a large stone and brick barn at the edge of the grounds of Thurnham Hall. The path continues directly before the Hall frontage. The rear part of the house is probably earlier than 1670 but this imposing Gothic facade was added in 1823; the Hall now serves as a Country Club. At the T junction with the entrance drive turn left towards the woods and the obvious spire of SS Thomas and Elizabeth RC Church. Although founded in 1785 this building was completed in 1848 and manages to look convincingly much older.

Beyond the gate take a stile immediately left and go down the field beside the wood. At the corner of the wood bear half left to a gate and then aim for bridge No.4 to regain the far side of the canal by a lock. The broad shoulders of the Bowland fells are clearly in view from behind Lancaster down to Preston. Bear diagonally half left and cross a long, narrow field to walk by the river Conder as far as a footbridge. Cross this and go half left again to the corner of the field. Use the gate nearest on the left, leaving the stone posts to your right, and walk straight ahead along and beyond the hedge line to a footbridge and stile. Turn right now up the field to the lane opposite Berry's Farm. Follow the lane left back to Conder Green and return to the start past The Stork.

# NICKY NOOK AND SCORTON

## WALK 5

★

4 miles (6.5 km)

OS Landranger 102

A place known as Nicky Nook ought, it seems to me, to be somewhere hidden, down in a valley and well out of the way. In fact it is just the opposite and could hardly be more obvious, for the cairn almost on the top of it is visible on the skyline of the Bowland fells for many miles as you drive north up the M6. How it got such an inappropriate-seeming name remains a complete mystery to me. What it provides is a short, sharp walk to the top, a magnificent view when you get there, and a delightful ramble back through the length of the Grize Dale valley.

The best start point is to park by the roadside at the junction of Higher Lane and Snow Hill Lane (GR: SD 511489) which climbs up the bank from the centre of Scorton village. The nearest motorway junction to Scorton is No.33 and the village can be approached by side roads from the A6 either from the Lancaster side or from Garstang.

Follow the path direct up the fell from opposite the road junction leaving the house called 'The Kennels' down on your right. Immediately behind you the lake in Wyresdale Park will be in view with the M6, the distinctive tower of Forton Services and the caravan park beside Winmarleigh bridge. After a short scramble up a steep bank of bracken and gorse you will pass a small reservoir on your right. As you come over the brow some old, and very wind-battered, Scots pine trees come into sight surrounded now by new planting and signs direct you on the

28

public path across the thin-soiled grass moor. Down on the left are a tarn and grouse shooting butts. The view east now opens up and the wide embayment of the Upper Wyre valley is visible from Clougha Pike and Ward's Stone round to the Bleasdale moors to the south. The clear path on the ground makes straight for the Ordnance Survey trig pillar at the highest point (705 ft). The cairn seen from the motorway turns out to be rather lower down and set in a field beyond walls to the west. The view out across the Fylde plain is very impressive and on clear days stretches all the way from the mountains of North Wales to those of the Lake District. Much nearer, and tucked close against a farm just beside Garstang, are the few remains of Greenhalgh castle.

Leave the trig point and head for the wall but turn right, down into Grize Dale, ignoring the large up-and-over stile. For a while the Barnacre and Grizedale Lea reservoirs are in view up on the moor on the far side of the valley but you drop rapidly down towards Grizedale reservoir surrounded by woods and plantations of European larch, birch, beech and sycamore. At the bottom,

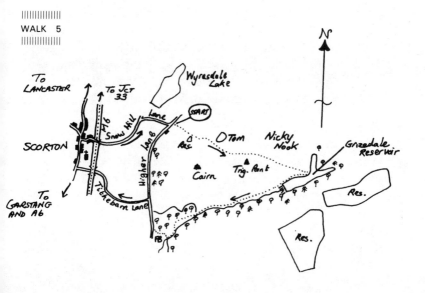

turn right along a bridle track. At several places there are rhododendrons amongst the trees and the track side is edged with gorse and decorated, in late spring, with the white of hawthorn blossom. Below the reservoir dam, alder and ash cling to the steep sides of the valley and the Grizedale brook tumbles over a small waterfall. In winter this area is a favourite feeding ground for flocks of blue, coal and great tits. The track eventually drops to stream level and the ground opens out on the right. Here, one day in late February, a small hawk flew swiftly up valley; could it have been the merlin which graces the Forest of Bowland AONB sign?

Rocky bluffs appear in the wood to the left and you need to turn right at the crossing of the paths, at a footbridge, to walk towards the massive beeches of Pedder's Wood. The view up valley with the autumn or winter sun on their russet leaves is especially fine. Shortly beyond this the path joins Higher Lane just below Slean End. Walk right along the lane to the junction with Tithebarn Lane and turn left, down to Scorton village. Turn right at the bottom and into the village centre past some handy toilets. Immediately across from the post office and shop is the Priory Café and a bar. The sandstone houses cluster prettily around the off-set crossroads. Slightly elevated is the church of St Peter, the edge of the churchyard touched by the motorway. A red-tiled roof to the nave and the small-slated spire make an odd contrast with the yellow sandstone of the walls. Complete the walk by continuing up Snow Hill Lane and over the motorway to pass the entrance to Wyresdale Park.

# PILLING AND KNOTT END

There are those occasions in the year when what we all need is a good blow, a chance to stride out for a short while, and an absence of serious ups and downs; this walk just fills that bill. It is also readily adjustable in length within the 6 miles. Much of the former Lancashire sea coast found itself under other jurisdiction at the reorganisation in 1974 and this is one of the few parts remaining formally within the county which is readily accessible. The contrast of the seasons is as sharp here as anywhere. Winter gales can make it impossible to walk the sea wall whilst summer sun may bake the stones and the reason for a collection of sky larks being called a 'charm' becomes very obvious indeed! At all times the sky is as wide as it can ever be.

The start may be at either end of the sea wall. My own choice is from the Pilling end at the car park beyond Fluke Hall (GR: SD 389500). Reach Pilling village (its church spire visible for miles around) along the A588 from Lancaster or via the side lanes west of the A6 just north of Garstang and turn along Fluke Hall Lane at The Ship pub and restaurant. (The alternative is from the car park by the ferry in Knott End village most easily reached from the A6 by A586 to A588 and B5377 – note that Shard Bridge over the river Wyre is still a toll bridge.)

Go up on to the sea wall and walk west. If you want to go through to the mouth of the river Wyre, opposite Fleetwood, you will continue all the way straight ahead without turning off the wall. Seaward lies the wide expanse of Preesall Sands and the

31

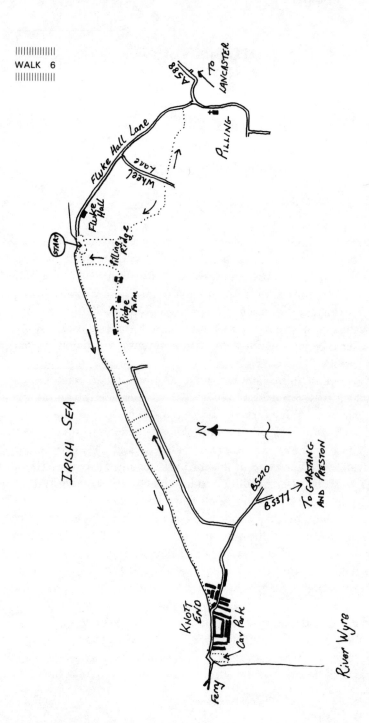

mountains of the Lake District sit on the northern horizon. There is access to the beach at several points without having to clamber over the massive limestone boulders which have been used to rebuild the wall in recent years. Do, however, take the warning notices seriously; as with much of the coast of Lancashire, the tides run in very swiftly and there are deep channels so it is all too easy to be cut off out on the sands. A very sensible precaution is to check the time of high tide with Fleetwood Tourist Office (Tel: 0253 773593). With the tide in, there are always sea birds to observe.

On the landward side the fields are drained; part way along you will pass the Preesall Pumping Station of the National Rivers Authority. Nonetheless, the ground remains marshy and often has standing water. The drainage ditches are overhung by wind-blown thorn trees. Curlew, redshank, and oystercatcher remain through the winter and retreat on to these fields as the tide comes in, leaving the sea to rafts of shelduck and the gulls. At several points it is possible to turn inland to join Pilling Lane and shorten the route; the Bowland fells fill the view. The last of these cut-offs before reaching Knott End itself is on a path beside a caravan park along a ditch overhung with willows and with its sides boarded up to prevent collapse. On the seaward side of the wall is a small remnant of saltmarsh.

Knott End is a mini-resort which is linked, across the mouth of the river Wyre, by a ferry which runs half-hourly between April and October (weather and tide permitting). There is a choice of shops and refreshments. Since the ferry is but a five minute crossing you might give yourself the additional fun of making the trip and spending a little time in Fleetwood itself. Originally laid out by Sir Peter Hesketh-Fleetwood, of Rossall, as a port served by the railway which began at London's Euston station, it had a few years of great success as a main route to Scotland. The completion of the west coast main line through Carlisle soon ended that and Fleetwood turned to the Isle of Man ferry, fishing, and tourists. Now the first of these is gone, and the second almost so. The town's story is told in the museum in Dock Street.

Make your way back either along the main road through Knott End to turn left into Pilling Lane or, if you have not gone as far as the village, turn left as your path joins Pilling Lane. There is a footway as far as Bibby's Farm passing one or two old cottages. The footway starts again at Beach Road and you will pass an interesting barn at Thornton House with its lower walls made entirely of beach pebbles. Aberdeen View (rather optimistic that!) is dated 1899 but the old school building, labelled 'Carter's Charity School' seems, sadly, to be undated. Leave the lane at the right-angled bend onto a surfaced track.

Keep directly ahead on to a farm track with the spire of Pilling church standing out half right. Pass 'Seafield' and Ridge Cottages on your left and a few chalets and caravans and leave the buildings of Ridge Farm on your right to continue to the old stone buildings of Pilling Ridge and walk between them. This is, clearly, the oldest building in the immediate vicinity and stands on the slightest of elevations above the marshy fields around it. The ditch on the right of the access track has a remarkably rich growth of water plants; follow this track round to reach the start point once more.

A worthwhile addition uses the path which leaves the rear of the car park to cross the fields by Old Ridge and Wheel Lane to Pilling village. The church with the outstanding spire is St John the Baptist (1887) and has a most beautiful decorative use of different colours of sandstone in its walls. Perhaps even more fascinating, is the Old Church of 1717 which is reached by a surfaced path across a field from the churchyard. Round the corner, across the Broad Fleet Bridge, is a windmill tower recently restored and converted into a house. The village has a pub, a shop, a restaurant, and toilets.

# LYTHAM

## WALK 7

★

4 miles (6.5 km)

OS Landranger 102

At first sight the massive works of British Aerospace at Warton and the long frontage of Blackpool, St Annes, and Lytham seem to make the northern side of the Ribble estuary an unlikely place for a worthwhile walk. Like many other places in the county, however, a closer look reveals details which deserve your time. Unusually, also, this walk is practicable in everyday footwear for much of it is on surfaced footway and the sandy nature of the soil means that even the part that is not drains quickly after rain. The windmill is an outstanding feature and is one of only two fully restored windmills remaining in the north-west of England (the other is at nearby Marsh Mill-in-Wyre, Thornton Cleveleys, near Fleetwood).

Use the A584 to reach Lytham. There is a clear choice of parking at either Fairhaven Lake or, and this would be my own preference, on the green beside the lifeboat station in Lytham and opposite the Queen's Hotel. The walk is described from this point (GR: SD 370270).

Begin by turning towards the Ribble Cruising Club and the café. The lifeboat station itself has a small shop in support of the RNLI. Over the sea wall is a stretch of saltmarsh and, in the right season and with the tide out, it is quite practicable to walk dryshod for 300 yards' or so before coming up on to the Promenade again. Here there is a free Lifeboat Museum in the old lifeboat station and beside it the windmill which is such a feature of this part of the shore and of the view from the south across the water from Southport. Built by Richard Cookson

WALK 7

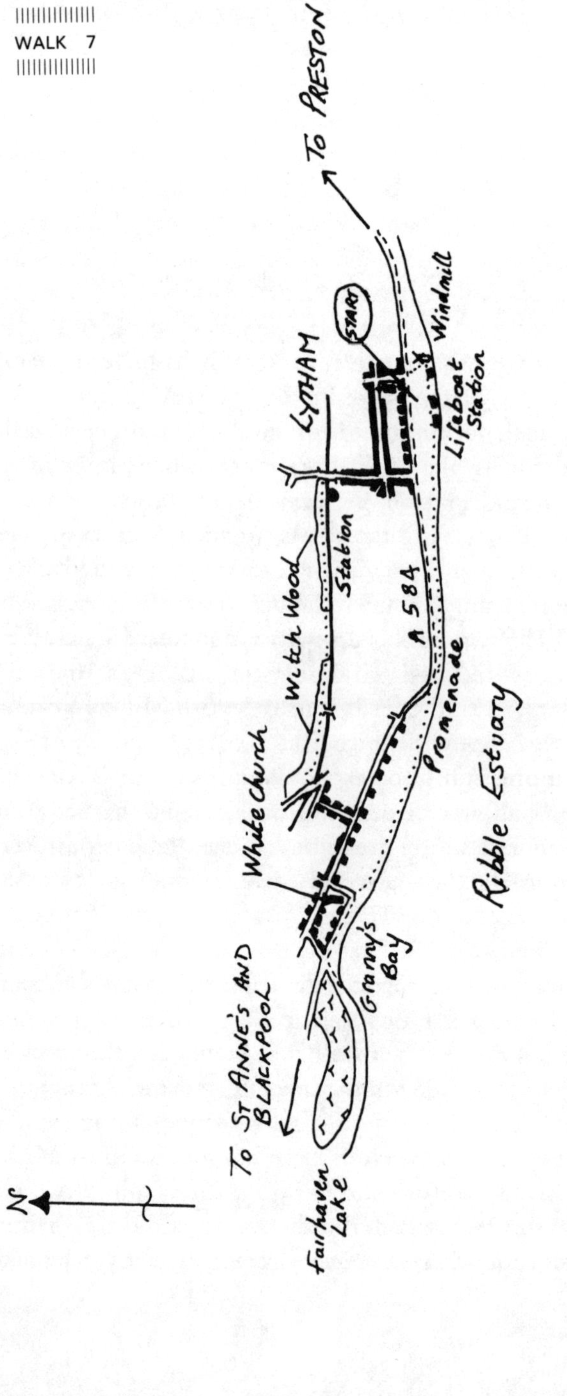

To PRESTON

LYTHAM

START

Windmill

Lifeboat Station

Witch Wood

Station

A 584

Promenade

White Church

Granny's Bay

Ribble Estuary

To St Anne's and Blackpool

Fairhaven Lake

N

in 1805 this former corn-mill was refurbished in 1988-89 by the local Council and is now open as an information centre with a display about the past of the mill (it is closed on Monday and Friday). Close beside the toilets is an information board about the Ribble Marshes National Nature Reserve.

Turn inland and use the diagonal path to the main road, crossing then to Station Road and walking to the corner of Clifton Street; turn left along the side of St Peter's RC church. The street is lined with shops and cafés with the 'Library & Lytham Institute: 1887' about half way along on the right. Most of this building represents mid-Victorian development after the railway arrived in 1846. At the far end you enter Clifton Square with a county information centre on the far side; turn right up Park Street to pass the Corinthian columns of an imposing Methodist church and go over the railway bridge by the station.

Immediately on the left is a path which heads along beside the railway and through Witch Wood. There are notices which remind you that this is a permissive path though this is a legal nicety since it actually now belongs to the local Civic Society. The wood is hemmed in by the railway on the one side and housing on the other but its oak, beech, sycamore and willow are large enough and its ground cover extensive enough, to give the impression of being far away from the bustle of the town. About half way through you will pass the cricket ground on the left and a school on the right. Continue ahead past a brick bridge on your left to emerge eventually on Blackpool Road. Turn left back over the railway and immediately go right on Cambridge Road and take the first left past the turn-of-the-century semis of Eversleigh Road to reach the A584 again at the bottom. Turn right now along what has become Clifton Drive. At the traffic lights is the URC White Church. This is, most unusually, covered in glazed white tiles and Pevsner's *Buildings of England* records that 'it must have taken some courage to put up such a building' – all I can say is that it takes all tastes and I quite like it!

At the next corner there is an old bus shelter with an incongruous Lakeland greenslate roof on a brick base. Bear left here and walk down to the corner of Fairhaven Lake. A variety of organised leisure is available here but it is, perhaps, more interesting in the winter for the waterfowl which are to be found upon it. Immediately on the Lytham side is Granny's Bay with a small patch of rather unhappy-looking saltmarsh. This unprepossessing spot is another area of great attraction for birds including ringed plover, sanderling, terns and waders.

Walk along and join the end of the Promenade. For over half a mile this follows the line of the former sand dunes with the houses set well back from the shore. Although the area gets badly trampled it does, nonetheless, still show a variety of dune-loving plants in flower in the appropriate season. At the end of this section, opposite the YMCA sports ground, a collection of old boats and tractors bears witness to the fading shrimping and fishing industry of the estuary. Return to the start by continuing along the Promenade past Lowther Gardens, a park with leisure and refreshment facilities.

# GARSTANG

## WALK 8

★

3 miles (5 km)

OS Landranger 102

The plain known as the Fylde, which borders the sea and the hills between Preston and Lancaster, is low-lying and marshy for much of its extent and, consequently, the centres of population are, even today, located on the drier ridges. After the Norman Conquest the Fylde was ruled under Lancaster from Kirkham, Poulton and Garstang. Of the three, the latter retains best its feel of the past, especially since both A6 and M6 pass it by. The walk takes you first out into the surrounding fields and returns via the canal to look at some of the more interesting buildings in the town.

Approach from the A6 and use the car park behind the Council Offices at the junction of Lancaster Road and High Street at the northern end of the town centre (GR: SD 493454). In the offices are an information centre and a discovery centre with displays about the history and natural history of Wyre Borough.

Follow the sign which points to the 'Riverside Walk' beside the river Wyre and turn left along the bank amongst the picnic tables and well-fed ducks. A flagged path circuits round a cricket field and leads you to a new concrete bridge. Use the steps on the left which take you up onto the track of the former Pilling branch-line from the main railway which runs beside the M6 about a mile east of here. From the top of the bridge you will be able to see the massive flood-control gates which were installed after disastrous flash-floods caused considerable damage downstream around St Michael's on Wyre.

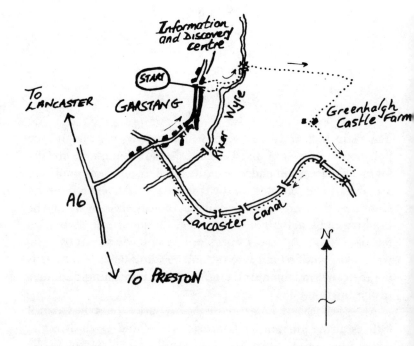

Turn across the river and follow the yellow-arrowed path along the old railway bed to go under the power lines which 'fry' noisily in damp weather. Up to the left the cairn on Nicky Nook stands out on the edge of the fells. Just before the stile in the bottom of the cutting turn up the bank on the right to a stile into the field. Cross this and join a track which bends to come round to the yard of Greenhalgh Castle Farm. What little remains of the castle is on the mound on the far side. Licence to crenellate (ie permission to turn it into a genuine fortress) was not given to the Earl of Derby until as late as 1490 but a good job must have been done because it shares the distinction of being one of the last two castles in Lancashire to have been taken by the Parliamentary army in the Civil War (the other was Lathom).

40

Having had a look at the castle, return to beside the farmhouse and walk south-east along the track for the length of two fields, turning right at the crossing of tracks to come to bridge No.56 over the Lancaster Canal. Join the towpath to your right and follow it along past the fishermen in quiet battle with their unseen quarry. At Dimples Bridge (No.58) there are moorings and a British Waterways information board; the barge *Rose Bud* lived up to its name, I saw, with a brave show of flowers in troughs on its roof. Just after bridge No.60 a milestone indicates that Preston is 17 miles behind you and then the canal itself is suddenly on a bridge over the river. This fine, plainly classical aqueduct was built by John Rennie in 1792 – the span is 100 ft and the clearance above the river 34 ft. A set of wooden steps to the left allows you to see the structure from below; unfortunately the vegetation along the river banks prevents a good clear view of the whole. Return up the steps and walk forward 100 yards to opposite the Garstang canal basin (there is another information board here). This formerly provided stabling and warehousing and there were small lime kilns.

At bridge No.62 go up on to Church Street and cross over the canal (beware of the traffic on the narrow bridge!). On the right, between the road and the canal basin is the old school (1845) and the Tithe Barn. This latter is the last of a long line of such buildings which have stood here since at least 1500, and is now a pub, restaurant and agricultural museum. Further along the street is St Thomas's church of 1770. Before this Garstang was served by a church 3 miles away in Churchtown which was certainly there in the early 13th century. Opposite the church are three Georgian cottages, two of them with doorways under one pediment. Directly ahead you will cross past a modern mini-roundabout and soon enter the old market place. The market charter was granted to the abbot of Cockersand Abbey by Edward II in 1310. The existing column replaced the old market cross in 1754. Many of the buildings of High Street, round to the left, are of considerable age. The Town Hall, in a Lancashire version of classical, dates from

1680 and was reconstructed after fire in 1750. Across from the modern box-like Council Offices stands the Old Grammar School; founded in 1756 it now serves as an Arts Centre. The car park entrance returns you to the start.

# INGLEWHITE AND
# THE BROCK VALLEY

WALK 9

★

4 miles (6.5 km)

OS Landranger 102

A series of more or less wooded valleys run down from the bleak fells of Bowland towards the Fylde plain between Lancaster and Preston. From the north they are Wyresdale, Grize Dale, Calder Vale, and the valley through which this walk passes, that of the river Brock. The middle ground between the mosses and the fell slopes rises only gradually towards the hills and much of it lies at only about 300 ft above sea level. Most of the farms are stock-raising and dairying holdings. The fine-textured soils are of a sort widely distributed throughout the county and tend to get rather wet and clarty in the winter months. Villages seem to be few and far between perhaps because, in the distant past, much of the area was attached to lower lying parishes like Kirkham, out across the Fylde. Inglewhite, as a consequence, is signed from miles around and is easily reached from either the A6 or the B5269.

Parking is available on the village green (GR: SD 547399). On the southern exit is The Green Man and the post office (actually 1 ½ miles up the lane to the north at Eccles Moss Farm) also supplies refreshments, even on freezing cold winter days! The green is surrounded by a delightful variety of buildings with a cross which marks the site of former cattle and sheep fairs, and on the side of a small building by the parish council noticeboard is one of the pre-war yellow and black AA signs which records Garstang as 6, Preston 7 ½ and London 220 ½ miles away.

43

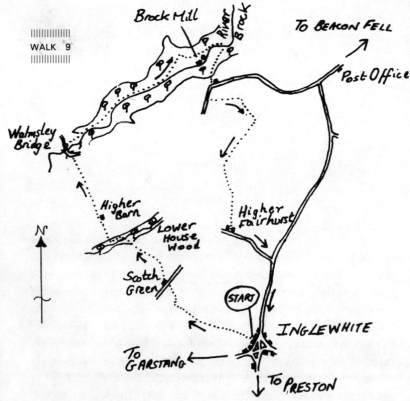

Leave Inglewhite green through the farmyard on the western side (there is no sign here) to join a track into the fields. Bear right a little to keep the hedge and ditch on your left and walk the length of two fields and at the corner go right for 20 yards to a stile. Cross a third field half right to a stile on the lane opposite the thatched farm of Scotch Green. A ladder stile enters the farmyard. In another 10 yards take the stile on the right and go round the buildings and an orchard. Follow the hedge on the right to a footbridge in Lower House Wood. Cross this and take the stile on the right into a narrow field and go to the left to a gate and a bend in a track. Walk right now to pass to the left of the large stone Higher Barn and move directly ahead across a large field to a stile just right of a pond and pylon. Drop slightly to a lane and down left to Walmsley Bridge (1883) over the river Brock.

44

Turn right over the bridge on a footpath signed to Brock picnic area and marked with a yellow dot. The good path on the bank of the river to the right passes through fields and woods and the valley quickly narrows. The stream tumbles over rock beds dipping slightly downstream. I stood here and watched flocks of tits working their way through the upper canopy of the alders whilst a tree creeper assiduously followed, circling the lower trunks, and a jay broke through with its harsh scolding from the far bank. At the next sign keep right and, in less than 200 yards, go right a short way to the ruins of Brock Mill, once quite a substantial concern. Retrace your steps to the track and continue upstream to recross the river by a large footbridge.

Bear left now, up the bank along an old eroded track amongst the tall beech trees of Gill Wood to exit on to a lane at a right-angled bend. Walk right for 50 yards and go left through a steel gate opposite the entrance to Throstle Nest (there is no footpath sign here). Follow the left hand boundary past a pond up to your right and bear right with the hedge until you come to a stile on the left. Do not cross this but turn at right angles away from it across the field and head for the large alder tree by a gate about 20 yards beyond the angle of fence and hedge. Bear left of the quarry mounds in the far field to a gateway. Once through this, aim half left past the hedge corner on your left and a quarry hole on the right to join a grassed lane leading up to High Fairhurst where you cross the yard to the lane. Return to the start by walking left and then right on Button Lane, named after the old Button Mill which you pass as you re-enter Inglewhite green.

# HURST GREEN AND STONYHURST

## WALK 10

★

3¼ miles (5.25 km)

OS Landranger 103

There are many places on the slopes of the Lancashire part of the Ribble valley which attract by their simple, straightforward, combination of houses and layout without either being especially pretty or being in danger of going over the top by deliberately trying to lure the visitor. Hurst Green is one of these and, particularly at weekends, gets its quota of aficionados who happily stroll round its mini-green and up towards the driveway which gives the standard view of the buildings of Stonyhurst College. The suggested walk, without being any great length, takes you deeper into some pleasant surroundings and looks at the college from different angles.

The village is on the B6243 and is best approached from Longridge or by the B6246 from Whalley. Roadside parking is available just up from the green beside the toilets (GR: SD 685380).

Start from the top of the green up Warren Fold and pass Whitehall Crafts and a row of cottages to enter a short green lane and go into the field; already the towers of the college can be seen above the trees ahead. Follow the left hand wall and take the gateway ahead at the corner of the field. Walk the length of the hedge on the left as far as an old iron kissing-gate and turn right on the near side of the hedge in front of you along the length of a games field on the far side. Pass through two similar iron kissing-gates to the corner of the wood in the dip. The view is of the ever-present Pendle and the incongruous brick

46

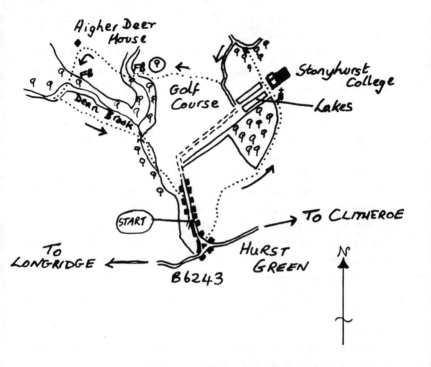

pavilion slightly right. The public path edges gently away from the wood to reach an iron gate in the corner on the right just below the domed building which houses the college observatory – a rarity anywhere and more especially so for a public school. The lane leads you past the college chapel and to the front of the main buildings.

All that could be said about Stonyhurst would take a book to itself and there is only space here to indicate some of the interest. The buildings grew out of the house of the Shireburns who were Lords of the Manor by the late 14th century. The next three centuries saw a variety of extensions and alterations until

47

the place passed into the hands of Thomas Weld who offered it to the Jesuits as a replacement for the English College at St Omer (France) in 1794. A very detailed description of the architecture is to be found in Pevsner's *Buildings of England,* but anyone can appreciate the unity which has been achieved over the centuries and the brilliance of the concept of the lakes which parallel the driveway. Stonyhurst is, of course, a functioning school so opportunities to view the buildings in detail are limited but in recent years it has been opened to visitors on afternoons in August (tel 0254 826345 to check current arrangements).

Once you have enjoyed the architecture to the full, move off again from the front of the gateway up the driveway beneath copper beech, horse chestnut and ash, at right angles to the lakes to reach a lane beside a gatehouse. Bear left and go left again in 100 yards. Fine views of the college can be had between the parkland trees on the left. Drop a little and, at the bend, follow the footpath sign to the right to enter the golf course which lies within the former deer-park. The path bisects tees 1 and 10 and crosses a fairway to continue below the round wood on the brow to the right. Cross to the valley wooded with beech, larch and spruce and walk up the fence to beside the 4th tee. A stile in the corner leads to a new footbridge across the stream and to a track to Higher Deer House. Bear left between the small brick outhouse and the large barn and angle slightly further left to cross the field to enter a wood of pine and larch. The path drops and crosses another footbridge and climbs sharply up to a narrow field. Bear right outside the wood edge to exit from the field onto a farm lane at the end of a wall where part of the valley woodland has been clear-felled.

Turn left and, in 50 yards, bear left along the wall. As you pass Hill Farm to the right you re-enter the woods and drop down to a bridge over Dean Brook. Just above the bridge, and for several hundred yards below it, the water has produced waterfalls like the Yorkshire Dales fosses and there are many potholes produced by the rotating wear of pebbles trapped in cavities in the rocks. The ground is typically almost bare of vegetation under large beech trees but the wood rings to the sound of wren, robin and other woodland birds. Stay on the main path as it rises left to become a track into the village. You emerge onto the street opposite the almshouses built by Henry Wise, gardener to James II, who also designed the college gardens. Turn right and go past the Bayley Arms to return to the start.

# DOWNHAM

## WALK 11

★

3 miles (5 km)

OS Landranger 103

Scattered up and down England a large handful of villages bid for the crown of most attractive. Far be it from me to make the choice but there can be no doubt that Downham is one of that handful. The village itself has a oneness which is outstanding and, from anywhere near the church or the Assheton Arms, the backdrop of the Big End of Pendle makes it visually unique in the North. At the same time, it's a place which always seems to have an ability to carry on its own life without being destroyed by its multitude of admirers. Undoubtedly, its success is closely bound up with the continuous occupation of the Hall by the Assheton family (now the Lords Clitheroe) since they acquired the manor after the dissolution of Whalley Abbey by Henry VIII. The whole is living testimony to the positive side of English family estates through the centuries. Sadly, on the northern horizon, land is in sight to which we are all still denied access, so bearing equal witness to the negative side.

Reach Downham by turning off the A59 Clitheroe bypass and going through Chatburn village. At the bottom of the village, just beyond the bridge, is a deservedly award-winning car park and stable block converted into toilets and information centre (GR: SD 785441). I can only speak for my own half of the toilets but they are certainly the cleanest, brightest and most surprisingly interesting I know of anywhere – don't pass by without looking in!

Walk the path to the Downham Beck by the bridge and cross the road on the same side to walk upstream. Some of the cottages on the left have flagged entrance paths spanning the stream and the flower display against the warm stone is fine at any time; I wish I could grow nasturtiums like these folk do. Food-bearing visitors, I suspect, make the stream a paradise for ducks and you have to be pretty hard-hearted not to respond to the resulting healthy mothers and broods dabbling its surface on a sunny day.

Pass into the field now and move along the bank; wild roses and hawthorn bloom and beds of watercress remind you that not all our watercourses are yet polluted beyond redemption. Follow the right hand fork of the stream and cross a shallow ford to take the left hand stile of two at the head of the field, the one in the short section of stone wall. Bear left to another similar stile in a short piece of wall but this one has wooden treads. Diagonally, across the field, is a further stile over a double fence and the Score Clough Beck on the far side requires a stride to cross. Move up between old stone gate posts beside a fine ash tree and walk up the left hand hedge to a stile beside a gate

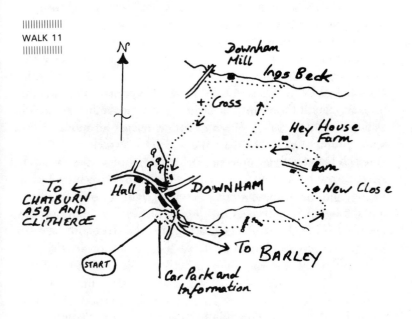

at the end of the wall. Just to the left is a rather decrepit squeeze stile and once over this aim for the gate to the left of the house at New Close and follow the right hand hedge up the field. The view to the left is dominated now by the twin limestone reef knolls of Gerna and Worsaw Hills. Through the gate at the top walk up past a spring to exit on to a lane by a converted barn.

A little to the left is alternative off-road parking for a couple of vehicles beside the entrance to Hey House. The footpath angles back to the right on an old track on a low ridge and beneath ash trees. A small abandoned quarry is half-filled with slurry. At the gate in the wall at the top, angle hard back across the field towards the farm buildings to find a stile in the wall close beside the near point of the triangular garden. From here the view behind to Pendle is good and is open ahead up to the Yorkshire Dales. Walk along the right hand hedge for two fields to reach a stone stile and turn right downslope. The view is once again good, this time of the upper Ribble Valley. Drop slightly right and cross a small square field diagonally to find a little gate hidden behind a burnt tree bole. An obvious old route goes down to a footbridge over the Ings Beck.

Stay, however, on this side of the stream and turn down the quiet valley with a mixed wood of broadleaves on the far bank. Beside some limestone outcrops you will shortly pick up the course of an old leet and reach the now empty millpond beside Downham Mill. Water drips down on ferns and moss on the walls as you traverse the garden and exit on a track. Just before this reaches the lane there are the remains of a stile in a gap in the hedge on the left. Take this and walk up between the larger and smaller limestone knolls. Just to the right, through the gap, is the base of an old wayside cross. The path contours up the embayment of the large pasture towards the wood on the near skyline. As you come over the brow, bear right towards the left hand corner of the wood and drop along the wall towards the houses of the village. A small white gate beside some cottages gives access to a path which leads down to the road just left of the post office, where there is also a café (closed on Wednesdays). The present church is an early 1900s rebuilding on a site which has been in use since, at least, the late 1200s. A little beyond it is the entrance to Downham Hall. The original Elizabethan buildings have been much altered and most of what you see is early Victorian. Bear back down the village street to return to the start.

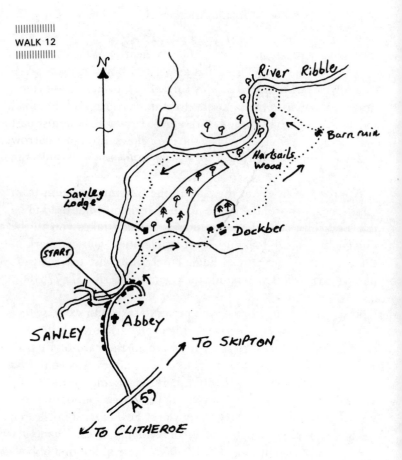

N

River Ribble

Barn ruin

Hartsails Wood

Sawley Lodge

Dockber

START

SAWLEY

✝ Abbey

TO SKIPTON

A59

TO CLITHEROE

# SAWLEY

## WALK 12

★

4 miles (6.5 km)

OS Landranger 103

The former existence of an abbey at nearby Whalley is well known and the church and the associated buildings still serve that town. The abbey at Sawley (or Salley), even in its heyday, never quite rose to the same stature and its ruins, and the small village, remain half-forgotten beside the river Ribble just east of Clitheroe. Above the village the river flows through a narrow valley – almost a gorge – for a while and this walk links the two.

Approach Sawley off the A59 in the Skipton direction from Clitheroe. A short lane to the north, a little on what used to be the Yorkshire side of the boundary, quickly takes you to the village. If you are making use of its facilities, you can park in the car park of the Spread Eagle hotel; otherwise use roadside parking across the road beside the river bank (GR: SD 776466).

Choose, first of all, whether you prefer to take your exercise first or to wander down to the river bridge and back towards the A59 to look at the abbey ruins. These are in the care of English Heritage and access to them is free. The abbey was colonised from Newminster, in Northumberland, being founded by William de Percy in 1147. It was never a rich foundation and was better known for its scholarly work. Few of its abbots came to national notice, though William of Rymyngton was Chancellor of Oxford University in 1372-73. It was one of the first abbeys to be suppressed by Henry VIII in 1536 and this contributed to the considerable distress in the North which led to the rebellion of the following year known as 'The Pilgrimage of Grace'. For a brief while the abbey was restored under William Trafford but he was executed in March 1537. His more magnificent colleague at Whalley suffered a similar fate not much later. The ruins were excavated in the 1840s by Lord de Grey and the strange gateway over the entrance to the nearby field is his doing and not a remnant of the former abbey buildings.

Your path starts at the back left hand corner of the hotel car park and bears left at the back of the rest home before going half right across the field past a limestone well trough to emerge onto a lane. Back down the valley the view is dominated by the cement works outside Clitheroe. Turn left to drop past banks of red campion, ramsons and jack-by-the-hedge to cottages hung with wisteria and to reach the lane along the river. Turn right at the bottom and go between the gateposts and up the metalled lane for 100 yards to a small gate on the brow on the right. Pass through this and a second one almost immediately to join the track up the valley of Skinners Syke. Up to the right are plantations and left, across the syke, the broadleaved woods and rhododendrons of the grounds of Sawley Lodge, the house being just visible down to the left. The small dam in the valley bottom is well silted up and green with algae in high summer. The track climbs slowly and bends left across the syke to rise to Dockber Cottages and the massive farm. Walk through between the outbuildings and the black and white farmhouse.

Continue the length of the first field and halfway along the second to a stile on the left over the fence. Diagonally left is a gate on the crest and slightly left through this a further gate at the junction of wall and fence on the far side of the field. The valley of the Skirden Beck opens to view on the left and the fells east of Pendle on the right. The faint line of an old track leads to a solitary stone post beside an ash tree at an old hedge line. Immediately to the left stands the ruined barn of Dockber Laithe; the path takes you round three sides of the building to lead you into the field which lies immediately to the left of the one you presently stand in. Drop down beside the hedge on the right to a stile and then aim just right of a dead tree to where a track crosses a gulley with a barn standing to the left. From this point bear half right to reach the bank of the Ribble opposite a cliff beside rapids at the top end of a bend. Ribble Way markers will be found here and a notice which reads 'Key farming and angling area. To help, please do not picnic on this stretch'.

Turn downstream past the fishermen's hut. Possibly, like myself, you will find a heron quietly getting on with his fishing job in the shallows close by. The river tumbles over dipping beds of sandstone and slips quietly through pools to riffles and rapids. The bank is lined with a great variety of trees – alder, sycamore, lime, beech, and hazel. Soon the path enters Hartsails Wood, loud with thrushes, robins, warblers and raucous jay in early summer. There are some damp stretches along the path here and the air is heavy with the garlic scent of ramsons in season. Down on the river mallard fuss and oystercatchers call. Out from the shade of the wood you walk first through fields along the river bank and then the path swings away left beside a large ditch rich with yellow flag, meadowsweet and spearmint. A long wood appears on the bank up to the left and a row of tall poplars marks the river across to the right. The path leads you through an area of parallel wide ditches, linked together and with the water level controlled by a sluice; my guess is this has been an attempt to farm fish or watercress. A series of rather steep-set ladder stiles now leads through to sheep pens and a dip trough at a track beside Sawley Lodge. Recross Skinners Syke and follow the track back to the gateposts and so along the lane to the centre of the village.

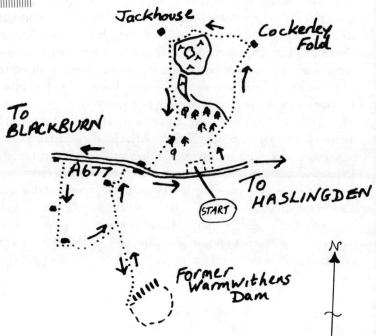

# OSWALDTWISTLE MOOR

WALK 13

★

2¾ miles (4.5 km)

OS Landranger 103

The bare northern flank of the West Pennine Moors rises on the southern edge of the District of Hyndburn centred on the detached urban area of Accrington, Oswaldtwistle and Church. Exposed though it is, it provides wide views to the north and is the ideal spot for a short stroll, particularly bracing on a crisp, sunny winter afternoon, preferably free of snow, but with frost on the ground.

Use the A677 which links the eastern end of Blackburn to Haslingden. About a mile west of the Coach and Horses is a car park, picnic site, and view indicator constructed by Oswaldtwistle Civic Society in 1985 (GR: SD 742253). Even from this lowish point on the hillside the view extends from Fairsnape and Longridge to the west, through Ingleborough, 32 miles to the north, and round to Pendle.

Some 20 yards in the Haslingden direction is a footpath sign marked 'Jackhouse'. Drop down to the field and keep left of the old culvert down to the edge of a plantation of larch, pine and beech and turn right along its edge to a stile by a metal gate in the field corner. Aim across to the buildings of Cockerley Fold with Jackhouse reservoir down to your left. The field before the house can be muddy. Use the gate on the left by the breeze-block barn. Go through the buildings and past the newly renovated stone house to bear left down the entrance road to a T junction. Turn left below the dam. On the left is a gate to the Jackhouse nature reserve where swans, geese and ducks will be found in the water at most times of the year. At the far end of the dam the old farm of Jackhouse itself lies just to the right. Climb slowly up left along the unmade track towards the top of the reservoir again. On this side there is much naturally seeded birch. At the top you will rejoin the main road opposite some cottages. The shortest circuit is to turn immediately left back to the car park.

Alternatively, turn right along the roadside verge to a footpath sign pointing up a track on the left a little before a white house with a wooden stable in the corner by the road. Turn up the hill and climb steadily into the invigorating wind which always seems to blow off the moor. Pass a farm first on the right and then reach a second on your left. Halfway up the field beyond this turn hard left, almost back on your tracks, to come down to a stile over the wall and head down to drop over a small syke and up onto a track coming down the moor. A diversion of ten minutes up and return takes you up to the dam of the now empty Warmwithens reservoir and an even finer view than you can get from the car park. A path leads up from here out onto the extremely wet and peaty moor and used to link over the top into Haslingden Grane. Return down the track, however, and continue to the farm buildings below and pass them to go right and left and down to the main road once more. Turn right along the verge on the far side to walk back to the car park.

# AROUND BARNOLDSWICK
# AND EARBY

WALK 14

★

5 miles (8 km)

OS Landranger 103

This has the same excitement as the 'Debatable Lands' of the Scottish Border for me. It is in between hill and valley, in between industry and agriculture, and is in between Lancashire and Yorkshire. It has been in both counties and is still of both so a foot across the boundary is well in order.

The pleasantest, and most convenient, starting point is Greenber Field Locks, the last locks in Lancashire and the highest set on the whole of the Leeds and Liverpool Canal (GR: SD 889482). British Waterways has, in recent years, created a picnic site here and there are toilets and a small shop which serves the leisure traffic on the canal. Approach from the A56 or the A59 via Barnoldswick centre or A59 from Thornton-in-Craven using the B6252 and taking the lane on the north side of the road after about 1¼ miles (2 km).

Take the towpath in the direction of Barnoldswick (pronounced more like 'Barnick') along the Pendle Way. All along this stretch, whatever the time of year, you will find pleasure craft moored, all sorts of boats and barges. Even in the depth of winter *Marsden Mist, Pakeleka, Champagne III,* and *Permanda* make you feel the soft, balmy days of high summer and the gentle pursuit of nothing in particular. A milestone records that Liverpool is 86 miles away, Leeds 41¼ miles.

Briefly, there was an abbey at Barnoldswick before the monks moved on to Kirkstall, near Leeds, in 1152. As you move on round the curve, the industrial edge of what became a cotton

61

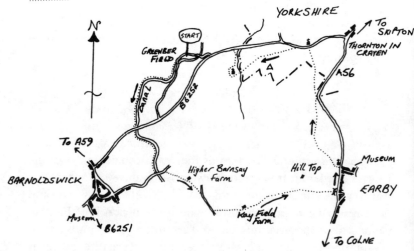

town, and now the home of Rolls Royce aero engines and Silentnight beds, is soon in sight. Follow the towpath to the second bridge (No.153) and leave the canal to cross over to the far bank. If there is time it is worth a 1¼ mile (2 km) detour in to Barnoldswick and back to visit Bancroft Mill in Gillians Lane off the B6251. When the mill closed in 1978 the 600 hp cross-compound steam engine was preserved and is on view, and under steam on occasion (times should be checked by telephone: 0282 865500 or 0282 813500/814586). There is an admission charge.

Once across the canal, walk up the rise to the corner and fork right on the 'private road' towards Higher Barnsay Farm and, taking the gate on the right in the fence just before the buildings, go ahead to the right of them to cross a field and rise again to join Salterforth Lane. As you turn right, look back on Barnoldswick in the valley: the contrast with the surrounding pasture land is most striking. At the first left turn to Kay Field Farm and as you pass the buildings take the middle of three paths to a gate and stile in the far corner of the field. Bear left now and use the right hand of two stiles by a gateway and edge right a little over the brow. Earby, a mini-version of Barnoldswick, is now in sight below. A gate takes you onto an old sunken track with a massive hedge on its right. Follow this down to join the track, coming up to Hill Top back to your left, and walk under the railway to exit on the A56. Go left 200 yards to the sign for the museum up School Lane.

The Mines Museum has exhibits of lead mining in the Pennine dales and is housed in the old, stone-built grammar school. Opening hours are, oddly, Thursday evenings and Sunday afternoons between the last Sunday in March and the last Sunday in October. For further information telephone: 0282 843210. There is an admission charge.

Return to the main road and cross over to pick up the Pendle Way again along the track beside the church. The path bears right across the fields to almost meet the main road again at a bend in about ½ mile and close to an old wind pump. Signs direct you almost due north over a hillock, crossing into Yorkshire at the wall by a small quarry, and dropping down past a well in the field to the road opposite St Mary's, Thornton-in-Craven. The spring show of snowdrops in the churchyard is one of the finest I have ever seen. Sadly, the church itself is kept locked and you would need to divert to the post office in Thornton to obtain the key.

Turn away from the village along the road verge for 100 yards to a stile on the left and then contour round the field below a trig point up to your left. As you move round the tower of St Mary le Gill will come into sight and you cross a small plantation and the golf course to drop to Gill Syke and, re-entering Lancashire, climb up to the church. This is the successor of that ancient abbey at Barnoldswick. Its oldest fabric is 13th century, the tower is 16th century, and the box pews and three-decker pulpit inside are 17th century. It is also kept locked. Beside it is what appears to be an old schoolroom inscribed 'MDCCCXXIV Mordaunt Barnard'.

Walk through the churchyard and round to drop back towards

Gill Syke and down to the road. Cross and then bear right down to the Greenber Field canal bridge to return to your starting point.

# WITCH COUNTRY

WALK 15

★

4 miles (6.5 km)

OS Landranger 103

Standing on top of the Big End of Pendle not only is there a round-the-compass view to be had on a clear day, but all that nearer country below, between Barley and Barrowford and Nelson, is spread before you. Here lived, amongst the lower folds of what was once the Forest of Pendle, that group of poor souls who became the victims of the prejudice of their time through the Lancaster Witch Trials of 1612. From the top of Pendle you can see and be seen for many miles and it is hardly surprising that this was the site of a warning beacon and that it should have become interwoven with the mixture of myth and truth which is today's tourist version of the tale of the Lancashire Witches. Each of the villages below makes what it can from the story – some more tastefully than others. This particular walk starts in the picturesque village of Barley and then circuits over the top of Pendle. It is probably the most challenging walk of all those suggested and certainly requires care to be taken over the weather. An alternative bad-weather route is also given.

Barley is best reached by side roads from the A6068 between Barrowford and Padiham, or round Pendle from Clitheroe via Downham. Park in the trust-the-motorist car park beside the White Hough Water; there is an information centre and refreshment kiosk with adjacent toilets (GR: SD 823403).

Cross the road by the village hall signed 'Barley Green' and take the marked bridleway towards Ogden Clough. Just beyond the multi-storey stone houses of Barley Green is the filtration plant of what was formerly the Nelson Corporation Waterworks (1910).

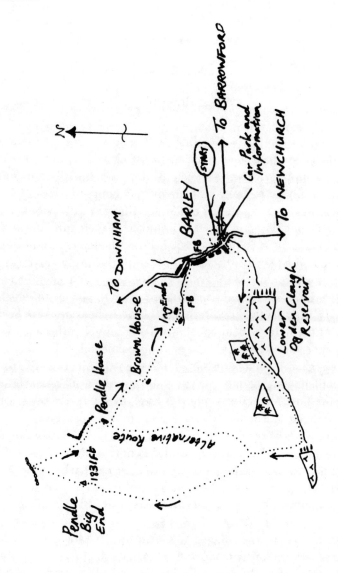

This is, in its turn, on the old site of a small cotton mill which operated until the 1880s. Follow the road up past a small plantation of pine, larch and spruce to the dam of the lower reservoir and walk along its side on the track. The reservoir was completed in 1914 and the plantations around it established in the 1930s. The new spillway of the upper dam stands out ahead. When you reach the top of the reservoir bear left at a Pendle Way sign (a witch on a broomstick!) and use this for the short distance up the valley bottom to a gate below the top dam. Ten yards up the track, before another gate, is a small bridleway gate to the right. Use this and climb quite steeply up beside the wall on your right. It is worth the (probably necessary) stop at the top of this section to lean on the gate above the farm of Buttock and admire the view back over Barley and the whole area which was famous for its cattle breeding in the late Middle Ages. An up-and-over stile takes you left onto the open hill.

In poor weather, with cloud or mist on Pendle, this is as far as those without a detailed map and a compass should venture. Under bad weather circumstances take the alternative of the track ahead to contour round below the steep slope of the Big End and rejoin the main route at Pendle House.

Although only one public right of way actually reaches the Big End of Pendle, the whole of this moorland area is open access and is criss-crossed with permissive paths and tracks. Take one such which bears off left up the bank from the stile and follow the faint path which gradually rises across the grass moor with its thin, peaty soil. Resist the temptation to be edged downwards by the slope and so work your way round the top of a clough which runs down to your right and eventually join a clear track which leads more gently up the ridge towards the summit. At the first cairn of stones a path drops off to the right and there is a signpost about 50 yards to the left. Continue ahead, however, past two more cairns to reach the trig point at the top at 1831 feet. Some love-sick swain has written his girl's name in stones in the eroded peat close beside – something of a contrast to the fictional imaginings of the death of witches on this very spot! The view on clear days is quite exceptional. Southport,

Ingleborough, Black Hambledon, and Winter Hill should all be quite readily distinguishable and the patient, with sufficient maps to hand, could easily fill in many more well-known landmarks 40 miles away, and more.

Leave the summit by walking forward towards the wall and turn right along it to pick up a very clear path which angles down the steep slope. Much of this has had stones laid carefully into the surface in recent years (called 'pitching') to reduce the erosion but, as you will see, the flow of water off the capping rock of Pendle Grit has resulted in even this major effort now requiring further attention. The path drops to the angle of the wall between Pendle Side and Pendle House. Follow it down towards the latter, to your right, and move right across the field behind the house to find a stile in the bottom wall. Descent of a long field brings you to Brown House and a clear path keeps to the left hand side of the stream lined with alder, sycamore, and crab apple in a little clough beyond it. Just to your right, at Ing Ends, is the Mirewater Trout Fishery, and for a short way you join the access road, with a rather wet 10 yards just beside the house. In 50 yards take the path over a footbridge to the right passing a sign saying 'Warning. Dogs chasing sheep will be shot', and follow the path down to emerge on the village street just right of the post office and opposite the Methodist Chapel. Walk right along the street, past The Barley Mow and the Pendle Inn (only built in 1930) and cross a footbridge left over the stream to the picnic site and so re-enter the car park.

# TOWNELEY HALL

WALK 16

★

2 ½ miles (4 km)

OS Landranger 103

In several of the former Lancashire industrial towns the Council worthies had the foresight to develop what have now become most valuable public facilities. Burnley's Towneley Hall and the surrounding woods and park came into the possession of the town by purchase in 1902. Today it is one of the finest free attractions in the whole of the North West. It is well worth allowing sufficient time to both walk and to visit the Hall.

The entrance to the park is off the A671 on the eastern side of the town centre and is clearly signed. Drive up the side of the river Calder past the High School and golf course and bear left to the main car park, perhaps a mile off the main road. Whether you choose to visit the Hall first or to walk, cross the bridge at the top right hand corner of the car park just below the nursery gardens (GR: SD 857312).

Follow the path beside the river upstream under the trees to reach a footbridge to the left beside sports fields. Cross back over the river and climb gently up beside a wood of sycamore, birch, ash and oak and follow the clear, arrowed, grassy track up the fields to the recently restored buildings at Cliviger Laithe. The view behind is across Burnley town centre and ahead is up on to Worsthorne Moor. Go through the first gate and turn immediately right through a second gate into the field.

Slightly left are some obvious old workings. Leave these just to your left and angle down the field to an iron kissing-gate in the wall. From the top of the bank the view is up the glacial channel of the Cliviger gorge and across to Deerplay Moor

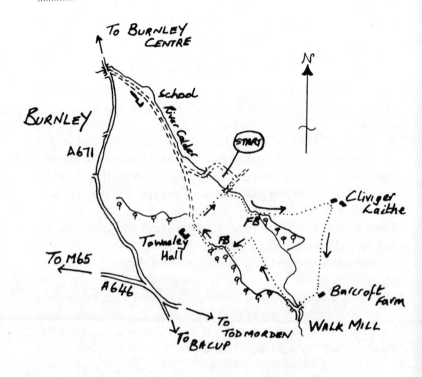

over the valley. Head down the field directly for the buildings of Barcroft. The front garden has a high wall with a unique archway over the entrance with dog-tooth decoration and dated 1636. I wonder if it was this building which was in mind, rather than the real Roughlee Hall, when Harrison Ainsworth wrote his novel *The Lancashire Witches*?

Bear right down the track now to recross the river once more at Cliviger Mill Bridge (which is in the hamlet, Walk Mill) and turn right amongst a group of modern bungalows to enter Towneley Park at the old East Gate. The path follows a ranch fence on the left to a kissing-gate onto the sports fields. Here, turn up left and work round to the left to join a woodland path at the footbridge in the corner of the wood. A gravelled path brings you, shortly, to the road which runs past the Hall itself and to alternative car parking. Return to the start by going down the broad double avenue of sycamores past the sports pavilion.

Towneley Hall now houses Burnley museum, a craft museum and the art gallery, and also has refreshment facilities. The Towneley family lived in it from the early 1400s until its sale to the town and made extensive changes to it over the centuries. The two-storied hall, built in 1725, is reputedly the finest room of that period in the county and is decorated with Italian plasterwork. There is also an Elizabethan long-gallery and a room totally furnished in Regency period. There is a good collection of paintings and furniture, and of Pilkington Royal Lancashire pottery. Local crafts and industries are displayed in the old brew-house and focus on Victorian and Edwardian Burnley. Temporary displays are changed about once a month. Nearby is a Natural History Centre with an aquarium and wildflower and geological gardens, and trails are laid out through the woods.

# HASLINGDEN GRANE

WALK 17

2 ¾ miles (4.5 km)

OS Landranger 103

The Grane Road from Blackburn, through Guide, towards Haslingden and Rossendale runs part way up the northern flank of the valley of Haslingden Grane and gives fine views on clear days. The valley itself is, however, worth a much closer look both in having attractive variations in scenery and as a good example of the way in which the past history of man in the area lies for all to read who are willing to spend a little time to do so. It is hardly believable now that over 1300 people lived here until the reservoirs resulted in depopulation.

Use the B6232 from either Haslingden or Blackburn and park at the old Clough Head quarry (GR: SD 751231). Here there are toilets and an information centre (open Wednesday and Saturday afternoons and Sundays and Bank Holidays between 10 am and 5 pm, from Easter to October).

Take the path at the bottom left hand corner of the car park and bear left slightly, crossing the site of a former brickworks as you go, and move up through a young plantation of spruce, alder and birch to join the route of the Rossendale Way beside a clump of large sycamores. Back across the valley the former Musberry Heights quarry, which produced setts, kerbs and flagstones until the 1920s, is clearly visible. Turn left past a ruin and along a substantial stone wall (6 ft high in many places) past a plantation of pines to a stile on your left. Nearby are the remains of the farm of Dole and some stone flags clamped on their edges to form a wall. Cross the wall and go down the field, keeping right of the gulley, to reach the road. Turn left now

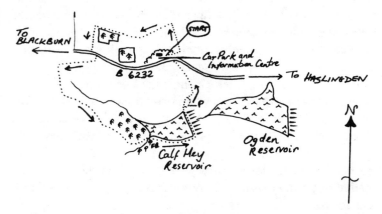

and, in 50 yards, cross over to a sign to the right, still on the
Rossendale Way.

Almost immediately the track bends to the right and should
be followed to drop slightly and bend back left below some
obvious old spoil heaps. Drop down to the stream in the Grane
with views over Calf Hey reservoir and Ogden reservoir to
Haslingden, Waterfoot, and Helmshore with Cribden Hill and
Cowpe Low beyond. Once across the stream climb up 20 yards
and turn left to walk the old track which linked up the now ruined
farms. Part of the track was paved with flagstones but peat and
soil have eroded into it and rushes have grown to obscure it and
cause many sections to be wet underfoot.

The track eventually reaches the top of a plantation and then
drops quickly slightly left into a wooded valley of one of the feeder
streams of the reservoir. Here you join the route of the Calf Hey
Trail (a leaflet is available from the information centre) at Point
6 and cross a footbridge over the stream. The woodland around
has been planted since the reservoir was constructed in the 1850s
and is largely fenced off to keep the sheep from grazing any
natural regeneration which comes in from the native oak, birch,
alder, and rowan still to be found in the steeper cloughs. When
the track brings you to the reservoir dam, turn across it. This

end of the dam is oddly wider than the far end because it had to be strengthened when it slipped during construction. The valley below contains two more reservoirs beneath which lie the remains of two mills. At the far end of the dam keep beside the wall and rise slightly to join a track through a gate. Immediately to your left are a couple of picnic tables with a pleasant view up the valley. Turn right, however, and walk past a stone trough which used to supply water for the village of Grane, and enter an alternative car park with an information board. This is the former site of Chapel Row and, at the far end, is the graveyard of the Methodist chapel which stood here between 1815 and 1955. A path to the left is signed to 'Clough Head'. Follow this up the small clough (do not turn over the stile to the left) to the road above and cross over to re-enter the car park from which you started.

A fine complement to a pleasant walk is to visit the Helmshore Textile Museums which lie along the B6214 in the village to the right at the bottom of the valley, only a little over 2 miles away. They are open weekday and Saturday afternoons all year, and from 11 am on Sundays between April and October. The museums, which have an entrance charge, have many working examples of machinery and detailed displays of Lancashire's involvement with the textile trade.

# THE HILE

WALK 18

★

3¾ miles (6 km)

OS Landranger 103

The words 'Forest of Rossendale' lie across the map over a plateau cut into by three valleys which run down from the north into the main Rossendale valley, the bottom of which is now occupied by a ribbon of urbanisation from Bacup to Rawtenstall. Even by the time the area became subject to the forest laws of the Norman kings and their successors it was already well depleted of trees. These laws were abolished in 1507 and small farmers were legally free to turn much of the land into cattle pastures in extension of a process which had already begun illegally long before. The area between the upper Irwell valley (a pre-Roman British name), to the east, and the valley of the Whitewell Brook, to the west, is typical of the outcome of several centuries of hard-won living by a breed of very independent farming communities. Because of the way the rock outcrops, quarrying of the uplands took place more to the south and west and so the country around the low hill of The Hile remains grazing land today. The walk is reasonably gentle and easy but, after rain, it may be wise to consider using wellingtons rather than shoes.

Although the area has many paths it is not easy to find convenient parking. I suggest starting up Bankside Lane off the A681, just west of the centre of Bacup – already 827 ft above sea level and the highest town in Lancashire. There is a car park on the left (which has a height-bar across the entrance) but you can continue up the bank and turn right up Maden Road to park at the Maden Recreation Ground (GR: SD 864227). The

75

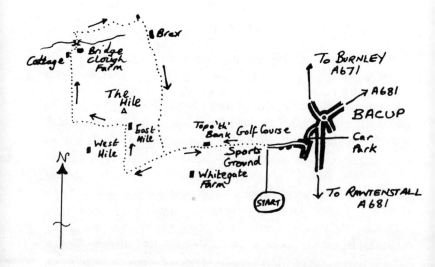

very existence of this here emphasises how little truly flat land there is in this vicinity.

From the Recreation Ground gates turn west along the track which runs between it and the golf course. At the white houses of Top o' th' Bank ahead walk through to the small gate at the far end of the buildings. Down to your left is Whitegate Farm and across the valley lie the massive workings of Great Moor, Britannia and Cragg quarries. Continue more or less directly ahead to cross a sunken track coming from the ruined Slip-in Farm to your right and use a stile to enter the fields. The track and path which continue straight ahead can be muddy after rain. Proceed for the length of six fields on your left to come to a clear,

76

stoned track which crosses at right angles. Turn right and walk up to beside the buildings of East Hile just below the summit (1160 ft) of The Hile which shows only as a low hill in the field above from this angle.

Turn left (west) now to pass a small area of building rubbish and join a track. Where this turns left to West Hile continue ahead along the right hand field boundary to reach the old route which comes up from Tunstead in the valley to your left. The view to the west takes in much of the West Pennine Moors between Bolton and Darwen. Turn right once more and pass a ruin, with a lone thorn tree growing out of it, and follow the obvious old trackway between broken down walls and newer wire fences. This section is rush-filled and wet in the bottom. Eventually you emerge beside a cottage just to the left of Bridge Clough Farm. Bear right and follow the track round across the clough and turn right at the junction to go first to an isolated cottage at the valley head and then turn right again through the farm called Brex. From here The Hile appears as a more definite hill with a double summit.

From Brex keep up to the left hand boundary and follow along the fields to come into a narrowed field end above Slip-in, down to your left. A stile in the right hand corner enables you to continue ahead to a gate into the field to the right. Use the stile beside this and drop back to your original track and turn left to return past Top o' the' Bank.

# SUNNYHURST AND TOCKHOLES

WALK 19

4½ miles (7 km)

OS Landranger 103

The Councils of many of the industrial towns of Lancashire have exhibited a predilection for the creation of attractive places over the years. Sunnyhurst Wood is one such felicitous spot, which is actually a commemoration of the coronation of Edward VII. In this walk the path through the wood is extended to link over the top to the scattered village of Tockholes in the adjacent Roddlesworth valley – though with a claimed 7 miles of path in the wood itself you might be tempted to stay there!

Approach the start off the main A666 about a mile north of Darwen centre, by using Falcon Avenue or Earnsdale Road to the left (west). Park beside the road; there is no parking in the wood itself (GR: SD 685233).

Enter either by the main gate on Falcon Avenue or by the track which leads down to the right halfway up Earnsdale Road. At the bottom of the track cross the bridge to the visitor centre. This is open in the afternoon on Tuesdays, Thursdays, and at weekends and displays temporary exhibitions about the wildlife of Sunnyhurst and the local history of the area. As a result of the development of the centre in recent years, a series of detailed booklets are available about the birds, flowers and trees which can, equally well, serve as an excellent background to the wildlife of the West Pennine area as a whole. Almost next door to the centre is a café and restaurant. Walk past this building and, at the next bridge, below a small lake, bear half right up the valley side and pass exposed small cliffs of sandstone intertwined with

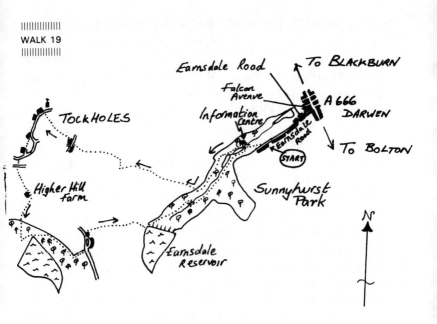

To BLACKBURN

Earnsdale Road

Falcon Avenue

Information Centre

A 666
DARWEN

TOCKHOLES

Earnsdale Road

To BOLTON

START

Sunnyhurst Park

Higher Hill Farm

Earnsdale Reservoir

N

the gnarled roots of beeches.

Stay on the higher path until you reach a field edge at a green iron gate. Walk slightly up between walls to pass the dairy of the farm on your left and the golf course on the right. Immediately behind, Darwen Tower is now in view on the skyline. Past the house a mill stone is set in the wall left of the gate and reads '. . ABELLA wife of DUXBURY' but there is no explanation to be seen. Go through the gate on the entrance track and up the brow to open up a magnificent view on a really clear day: Southport, the Lakeland fells, and Bowland may be visible and, more closely, Hoghton and Witton, beyond Blackburn. At the T junction a broken windpump stands to the left and – surprisingly – a herd of fallow deer may be seen grazing.

Turn right and admire the view again from the bend. Ingleborough stands out through the gap to the north and Winter Hill lies south, topped by its TV mast. Drop down now to the lane through Tockholes. To the left you will find the Victoria pub and to the right lies The Rock. Move in the latter direction past the front of the village hall and turn left immediately beside it past Silk Hall and down to Rose Cottage. A field gate on the right enables you to cross down to a stile in the right hand corner. A second, wooden stile under a birch tree leads you to a stone stile on to the lane opposite St Stephen's church. The claim that a church existed here in AD 640 is dubious but some building may well have been here by 1500 and the new church was built in 1965. Close beside is the old school building (1834) with its strange outdoor pulpit – the stone one replaced an earlier wooden one. In the graveyard is a fragment of a cross inscribed 'The upper portion of this monument is supposed to be a remnant of the old Parish Preaching Cross probably dating from 634. The lower portion is probably part of the ancient TOCHES stone from which the parish takes its name'.

Continue to the left past old Chapels Farm and go right over a stile at the second bend by Lodge Farm. Cross to a small gate and, bearing right to a stone stile between a cottage and barn, go down the track to the bridge. At the junction of tracks turn right and, in 30 paces, go left up a rather obscure path across the hay field behind a house and cross the track ahead to a wicket and stile to climb a little to Higher Hill Farm. Go across the track at the footpath sign and bear right to the corner of the garden wall. Halfway up the wall of the farm is a projecting garderobe – an early loo which would originally have had a pit below it.

Go steeply down the field now to an iron gate at the bottom into woods of birch, larch, sycamore and oak and follow the path down to cross the cascade from the Upper Roddlesworth dam. Bear left up to the top and cross back over the cascade. At the end of the dam go right and immediately left up a stepped path away from the reservoir edge and amongst pine trees. At the track and field gate go right inside the wood on a permissive path to reach the lane with another view of Darwen Tower ahead. If you need them, the Roddlesworth information centre and the Royal Arms are to the right. Continue by crossing the road by the information centre approach sign and go past the refurbished cottages and right along the lane for a few yards at the far end to Fine Peter's Farm (dated PME 1757).

A track round the far end of the farm runs to the right, up the brow, to a fine view south and east over Rossendale. As the path drops down towards Earnsdale reservoir it has been eroded into the soft shales exposed here and you pass beneath hollies and thorn bushes to reach the end of the dam. Here, at all seasons, you will find fishermen and waterfowl – the latter the unquiet part of the pairing. In addition to the ubiquitous mallard, there is a chance, in winter, of seeing coot, tufted duck, pochard and, more rarely, goldeneye and whooper swans.

Across the dam end is a green iron gate. Take the path through this, entering the woods again, and drop down to the bridge to the right in the valley bottom. Cross the stream and follow the path down the wood. Grey wagtail and dipper will be seen on the stream in season. There have been extensive plantings in the wood over the years and the list of trees extends to not less than a dozen conifers and about 45 broadleaved trees. The range of flowering native plants is extensive making it an excellent place in which to try a little gentle identification. Pass the stone-pillared bandstand which serves as a shelter to return to the bridge beside the visitor centre and thence make your way back to your start point.

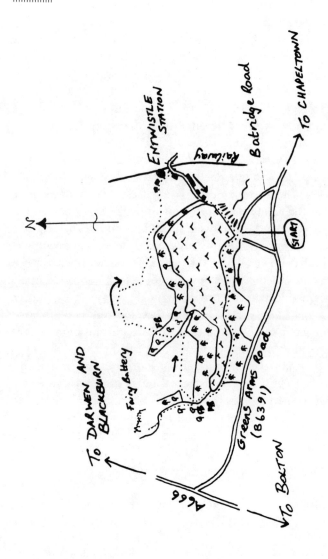

# TURTON AND ENTWISTLE RESERVOIR

WALK 20

★

3½ miles (5.5 km)

OS Landranger 109

The Pennine moorlands of Lancashire are peppered with reservoirs many of which will be seen during other walks described in this book. Few of them, however, are attractive enough to deserve a walk of their own but Turton and Entwistle reservoir is certainly an exception. It was originally built in 1838 to control the supply of water for bleachworks down the valley of the Bradshaw Brook. Later it was enlarged and is now part of a complex which serves the Bolton area.

The most convenient approach is off the summit of the A666 between Bolton and Darwen along Greens Arms Road. Two car parks lie close to each other at the south western end of the dam (GR: SD 722172). One is accessible along Batridge Road (although this then crosses the dam it is not a through route for cars) whilst the other is at the end of a new lane which leaves Greens Arms Road a few hundred yards west of Batridge Road. In either case, walk to the end of the dam and take the broad path along the southern side of the reservoir.

The plantations – on this side called Tarkingtons and, on the other, known as Fox Hill – are now well established and provide a delightful contrast of colour and texture with the water and the backdrop of Turton Moor at the reservoir head. Especially in the autumn, when the native birch and the beeches are changing colour, this man-made landscape is becoming almost as attractive as more famous examples, like Tarn Hows and High Dam, in the Lake District. Across from the footbridge over the Cadshaw brook at the head of the reservoir there is a solitary red oak which is set off particularly well by the more sombre conifers behind. In addition bilberry, heather, bracken, blackberry and rowan add their colour and delights. Over the footbridge is a patch of bright yellow gorse and the peat-stained water tumbles beside you over a series of small stone weirs.

A short diversion, along a permissive path up the valley, takes you to the Fairy Battery or Pulpit Rock. Here non-conformists met to worship in the years between 1664 and 1689, after which time chapels were permitted to be built.

Beside a second footbridge a stile leads into the field ahead. Take this and climb slightly left up towards the corner of a woodland. Right-angle right on a clear track as far as the remaining foundations of the buildings of Fox Hill. Holcombe Tower, a memorial to Sir Robert Peel, just stands up above the skyline ahead. Turn left and down to a stile into a beech wood in the clough and a footbridge over the stream. The path goes past the solitary pine amongst the beeches to a stile in the fence. Follow up the gulley on the left to a single sandstone gatepost with three holes in it and cross over to walk up the far side to a stile by a gate onto a track. From this point the whole sweep of the Pennines to the east of Greater Manchester comes into view.

Walk right along the track to the first stile on the right beside an iron gate on a bend. Drop down on an old, stony track between walls beneath beech and sycamore to a field gate. Bear left along the boundary and an old wall line to go left 50 yards beyond the end of the wall and cross a ditch and climb up the bank by a lone small sycamore. Contour round the knoll and pass a concrete drinking trough to reach a stile onto Edge Lane in the corner. Turn right and walk past New House Farm to the junction of tracks and the road beside Entwistle Station and the Strawbury Duck pub and restaurant. Pass this to Overshores Lane and go along a terrace of cottages to drop over the bank and down to the reservoir dam. Cross this to return to the start.

# JUMBLES

## WALK 21

★

3 miles (5 km)

OS Landranger 109

Jumbles is an unusual place. Unusual in that, so far, I have been unable to find an explanation for its odd name, unusual in having such a recently created reservoir, unusual in having a Country Park which straddles the boundary between Lancashire and Bolton, and unusual in this recent development having almost completely diverted the focus for visitors to the valley from Turton Tower to the valley bottom. The route of this walk however, links Jumbles and Turton Tower and will, hopefully, persuade you of the interest of this part of the urban fringe.

Access to the start is from the main Bolton to Ramsbottom road, A676, by turning left just below The Lamb inn. Park in the main car park by the toilets to the left (GR: SD 736139). The information centre will be found to the right (open on Wednesday and Saturday afternoons and Sundays and Bank Holidays between 10 am and 5 pm from Easter to October, and from 11.30 am on winter Sundays). In addition to the sale of leaflets and guides the centre has a display about the Jumbles area.

Begin by going north past the information centre, past a plaque recording the building of the reservoir in 1971. Its job is actually to provide compensation flow to the Bradshaw Brook so that drinking water can be taken in greater volume from the other reservoirs higher up the valley. Follow the well-surfaced path along the side of the reservoir. Along this section you will find the first twelve posts of a nature trail for which a leaflet is

86

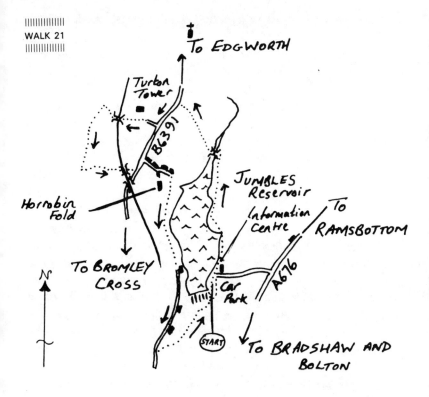

TO EDGWORTH

Turton Tower

B6391

Horrobin Fold

JUMBLES Reservoir

Information Centre

To RAMSBOTTOM

A676

N

TO BROMLEY CROSS

Car Park

START

TO BRADSHAW AND BOLTON

available. There is a considerable variety of planted trees and, just off to the right, is an open-access woodland bird hide. The water itself will certainly have several fishermen sitting beside it and a variety of waterfowl on its surface. Below the reservoir lie the remains of Horrobin Mill (pre-1780 to 1941) and the bay beside the Conservation Area was once the lodge which provided water power for its bleaching and dyeing operations. A little further along, and up a bank to the right, is another small lodge of the former mill beside which the attractive, bright-red, but poisonous fly agaric toadstool will be found growing in autumn. At the head of the reservoir cross the somewhat unattractive, but no doubt functional, iron and concrete bridge. As you do so a cross-section of the rocks is exposed to your right in an old quarry face. The layers of sandstone, shale, and coal deposits

87

laid down in a massive delta 300 million years ago are clearly to be seen.

Climb directly ahead through a plantation of larch and Scots pine and cross a conduit pipe. As you move up the field beyond, the spire of Turton parish church, St Anne's, at Chapeltown comes into view and the moorland beyond Edgworth provides a backdrop. Just before you reach the road (B6391) there is a well-preserved Second World War concrete pill-box. At the road, cross and turn left along the footway to the top of the brow and turn right at the sign for Turton Tower. One hundred yards up the driveway, overhung with beeches, stands the Tower which is now a Lancashire County Museum (opening hours are rather complicated but include afternoons – except Thursday and Friday – and it is closed in December and January. There is an entry charge. Tel: 0204 852203 to check). The building began as a defensive pele tower in the 15th century and was modified around 1600. During the Civil War it was used by Humphrey Chetham (the founder of Chetham's Hospital in Manchester – now a famous Music School) as a hostel for Roundhead troops. Victorian times saw refurbishment and romantic Gothic embellishment by the Kay family and, latterly, it served as the headquarters of the former Turton Council. It now has a tearoom and houses an interesting collection of furniture and armour and a variety of temporary exhibitions.

After your visit to Turton Tower, return to the driveway and turn right up the hill. Almost immediately you will find the waterwheel from the former Black Rock Mill which has been preserved beside the stone barn by the Local History Society. Beyond the barn the driveway crosses the single-track West Pennine line by a decorative castellated bridge. Built in 1848, the railway continues to link Bolton and Blackburn today. The driveway degenerates into a track now beside a small wood and up a shallow clough to a T junction at a wall. Take the stile by the gate on the left and continue beside the fence on the left. You will find that you are forced to walk round the decayed fence of a former plantation of trees. The effects of sheep grazing on their survival are very obvious. Aim now for the telegraph poles and reach a kissing-gate between two flags in a wall and enter a field. Take a stile to the left in the fence at the top of the brow by a Council notice which reads 'Please do not light fires'. The path goes down the slope through bilberry and heather and amongst birch, larch and alder to cross a stream and a field at the bottom before going under the railway in a tunnel and emerging onto the road again.

Cross the road and walk left over the bridge and turn right down Horrobin Lane with its relaid surface of stone setts. At the fork bear left for Lees Cottages past a small new development and some renovated buildings and turn right over one of the iron and concrete bridges to rejoin the path round the reservoir just behind the Civil Service Sailing Club. Up on your right is the renovated farm complex of Horrobin Fold. Once more you will find posts for the nature trail (numbers 13 to 16). The path is well surfaced and leads eventually through the stable yard at Grange Farm and on to the unmade Grange Road beneath an avenue of alternating limes and horse chestnuts. Pass a sign on the right to alternative car parking at Ouzel Nest and take the stile on the left into the field beyond the house with the large, newly created Italianate garden and drop down to the Bradshaw brook below the reservoir dam. A dipper was busily foraging here for water creatures as I crossed the brook. A path and steps past a house on the left lead up to the car park from which you started.

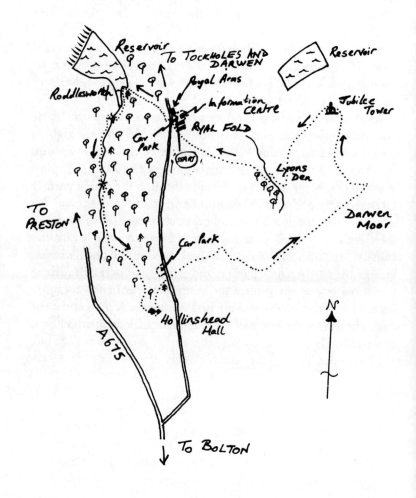

# RODDLESWORTH AND DARWEN MOOR

## WALK 22

★

5 miles (8 km)

OS Landranger 103

From a wide area of the West Pennine moors, the coastal plain, and much of the Ribble valley, the tower on Darwen Moor is a major landmark. The valley below it, to the west, in which the Roddlesworth reservoirs lie, is very attractive indeed. Though the main road tends to speed you past without revealing much of the interest which is so close to hand, a minor diversion will quickly bring you to one of Lancashire's most enjoyable areas. The walk described joins up the high moor with the valley bottom, but can be shortened along the lane if poor weather makes the former unattractive.

The easiest access is from the lane which runs east and north from the main A675, Bolton to Preston road. Alternatively, approach through Tockholes village from Blackburn. Park at the information centre beside the Royal Arms at Ryal Fold, which is open Wednesday and Saturday afternoons from Easter to October, and on Sundays and Bank Holidays (GR: SD 665215).

Begin across the road at the footpath sign opposite the bus turn-round where there is a map of the nature trail (a leaflet is available) which was opened as long ago as 1970 as the local Women's Institute contribution to European Conservation Year. Go back right towards the pub and walk along the trail route in reverse order from posts 8 to 4. The path through woodland of oak, sycamore, alder and willow is muddy and slippery after rain and, at the bottom, reaches the shores of the Upper

91

Roddlesworth reservoir amongst a group of pines – the reservoir is linked to the Rivington complex on the far side of Anglezarke Moor to the west. Cross the Roddlesworth brook on a concrete bridge and walk upstream. The ground flora is rich in season – dog's mercury, wood sorrel, bluebell and celandine, amongst others, and woodland birds are common. The peat-brown water comes tumbling down over low shelves of sandstone and forms magnificent icicles in winter. As you rise up the valley the vegetation slowly turns towards moorland and banks of woodrush give way to fine-leaved grasses and birch and holly become commoner. On the small cliffs mosses and liverworts grow in profusion in the damp atmosphere.

After post 4, cross back over the brook and continue upstream on a well-made track. The valley shallows and opens and the woods recede. Keep right over Slipper Lowe (named after the wooden brake shoes fitted to carts). On the top, on your right, there is an unusual recently coppiced area of alder. Over a stile and down between stone walls you suddenly come upon the ruins of Hollinshead Hall in a sheltered hollow. As early as 1380 it is recorded as the site of the manor house of Tockholes. The Hall appears to have been rebuilt in stone in 1776. It was demolished and left to decay for many years but was excavated and made safe in the early 1980s. At the far corner of the site is a well-house – sadly, now, usually kept locked – the water from which reputedly cures eye troubles. An information board gives some details of the Hall and its site.

Leave the Hall site at the rear left up an old track through the trees and rise up a shallow clough to a gate onto the Tockholes lane. (Return from here if weather or time dictate.) Cross the road onto a footpath signed to Lyons Den and walk over the field to a stile and the summer sound of larks and pipits. Ignore the path arrowed to the left and go up the zig-zags to a gate on to Darwen Moor. The tower is now in view to the left. Use the track which more or less contours above the clough to a gate and a seat on which to rest and enjoy the heather of the moor top. This is hallowed ground and the site of an early battle over the right of the townspeople to access for exercise and fresh air which they finally won in 1896!

Take the left hand track at the gate and, in a few yards, continue ahead over the top of the moor. Way to the east is the Peel Memorial tower on Holcombe Moor. Drop down a little. As you do so you almost look down the top of the massive chimney of the old India Mill – now a nest site of peregrine falcons. At the crossing of tracks turn left and contour round to Darwen Tower. This is a celebration of Queen Victoria's diamond jubilee in 1897. It was refurbished in 1972 and it is well worth the climb of the spiral stair to the lantern at the top and a look at the indicators of the view off the balcony – it stretches from Black Combe in the southern Lake District to Kinder Scout in the Peak.

Leave the tower past the trig point and go left with Sunnyhurst Hey reservoir below you. At the stile in the fence on the right drop steeply down the short bank into Stepback Clough by the remains of 'Old Aggies', once the site for teas. Cross to the left over the stream, which flows down from the former mine site in the clough, and swing round below the small wood on the steep bank. The soft shales continually slip to form terracettes on the hillside and some of the trees are acutely bent at the base as they have struggled to grow vertically against the push of the moving soil. At the end of the wood take the iron gate on the right and follow the track across the field back to Ryal Fold and the car park.

# WHITE COPPICE

## WALK 23

★

2¾ miles (4.5 km)

OS Landranger 102, 108 and 109

Tucked under the foot of the height of Great Hill at the northern end of the Anglezarke Moors, White Coppice is the epitome of rural England on a summer Sunday with cricket in progress on the cottage-fringed green beside the Goit. It shows how quickly things can change since, in the middle of last century, this was a thriving small industrial hamlet firstly with bleach works, then cotton mills and, later, the quarries for the reservoirs. However that may be it is, today, a quiet backwater frequented by those who are happy to enjoy the scene and take things easy.

Three OS map sheets are needed to find the way conveniently to White Coppice. The simplest route is from the A674 (either off the M61 Junction 8 or from Chorley town centre) just north east of Chorley up a lane signed to Heapey and White Coppice. Park either beside the cricket field up the unmade track at the end of the village or alongside the track (GR: SD 619190).

Walk up the left hand side of the cricket field beside the white cottages and turn left below a small dam, following the path to the right up to the top of it by the overflow leet. Once in the field, climb half right round The Lowe to the old wall and follow this round to reach Tootals Farm. Across to the right is the open Access Land of the West Pennine Moors Recreation Area. Walk between the buildings to a T junction of tracks and turn right and pass an old stone barn on the left. Turn left into a field at the left hand of two stiles. Healey Nab, crowned with plantations, rises to the left and the gas-holder of Southport, on the coast, is visible ahead. Keep left of the water trough to a stile by an

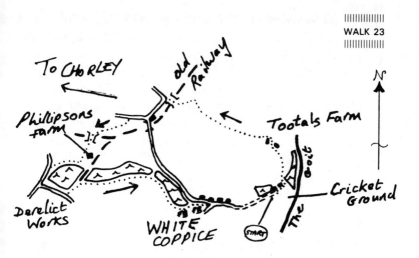

oak tree and cross the field diagonally to the right. Cross a further fence line and go left of the telephone lines to meet a track at the junction of an old hedge and ditch line with a bank. Bear right and drop down to a stile by the gate. Turn left on the track past Garstang Lane Farm and over the bridge of the former railway to walk to the bend of Chapel Lane.

Turn left and walk along to the road junction beside the Railway Inn at the end of Coppice Lane. Follow the Chorley sign along Tithe Barn Lane and go left in 50 yards at a footpath sign. Follow the field edge, ignoring the stile to the left, to a stone bridge and cross back over the old railway. Across the centre of Chorley is the Parbold-Ashurst-Billinge ridge, beyond that the tower of St Michael's at Aughton, near Ormskirk and, on really clear days, the mountains of North Wales in the distance. Follow the path down a shallow valley between wire fences with Philipsons Farm up to the left until you join the metalled lane beside a reservoir and turn right. At the road, bear left 50 yards down to the junction below the dam and turn left along Higherhouse Lane for 100 yards. Opposite the entrance of the former works turn left up the bank at the far end of the dam and right up the steps to a fishermen's car park on the old railway line bed. Use the stile and take the track along the bank of the middle reservoir. Great-crested grebes breed here, and a variety of multi-coloured ducks are to be found, together with gulls and terns and swooping damsel flies.

Continue through the fields beside the higher reservoir until you reach a footbridge across the inlet stream. Cross this and a further footbridge beside some picnic tables and a seat opposite Warth Farm. You will find the cricket club fixtures posted on its wall in summer. Walk up past a ford and some cottages with finely kept gardens on the left to pass No.6 Lodge and return to the cricket field.

# WITHNELL FOLD

WALK 24

★

2 ½  miles (4 km)

OS Landranger 102

The Leeds and Liverpool canal not only linked those two great urban centres and the smaller ones between but, in the years after its completion in 1816, enabled a variety of smaller enterprises to flourish in a much more rural setting. What is now the largely dormitory village of Withnell Fold is just such a place which has gradually edged back towards its rural origins over the years. The route of this walk passes two more of the several places including 'fold' in the name in the immediate area and provides an opportunity to visit one of several examples of a nature reserve developed from an industrial site.

Withnell Fold is signed from the main A674 along a narrow lane just on the Blackburn side of Higher Wheelton on the road to Chorley. Drive down to the T junction at the bottom and turn right over the bridge to park beside the canal bridge just below the chimney (GR: SD 611231).

Start by having a look at the variety of small businesses which now occupy the remaining buildings of the former paper mill (1844). Most of the other buildings on the opposite side of the entrance track have now been demolished though a few, including the former Reading Room, have been converted to domestic use. Cross over the stone canal bridge and walk along the towpath in the Blackburn direction. Very quickly all signs of industry are left behind and you move into fields accompanied by ducks, coot and moorhens. Across to the left is the wooded rise on which Hoghton Tower stands. By the second stone bridge is a stile on the left. Use this and cross back over the canal to

97

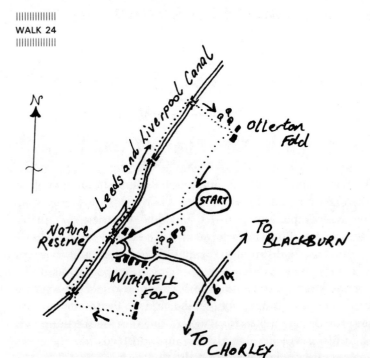

a very high stile on the far side. The path rises up between fences – where once there were hedges – to pass the side of a small wood and bear right before the buildings of Ollerton Fold. Almost certainly, each of these 'fold' named farms was so called from its use as a cattle-breeding site as, indeed, many still are.

The left hand of a pair of steel gates is arrowed for the path. Ahead, the mill chimney stands out and it is clear that the canal passes through a narrowing of the valley at Withnell Fold. To the right Brinscall church is visible. Cross the fields along the right hand fence line to drop to a stream below the former mill reservoir wall with an iron railing on top of it. Bear half left now, up to the corner of the wood with the reservoir down to the right. Through the gates a track leads along the side of the wooded gardens of Withnell Fold Hall to emerge at the top of the village beside a farm building marked IEH 1736.

The setts, or cobbles, of the village street have been retained here (and have recently been relaid). Down on the right a facsimile of the village stocks stands beside the entrance to a memorial garden. Return a little uphill to the track which starts beside 'Oakbank'. This passes below one of the old mill lodges, which ensured continuous water supply, and then the sports field where you may find a small amount of alternative parking. Take the iron gate ahead and cross the field past a pond. At the buildings of Brandwood Fold turn first right on the track before the shed on the right and walk down the valley of the Flash brook. The stream side is painted pink by Himalayan balsam when in bloom. A five-arch aqueduct carries water from Thirlmere, 65 miles away in the Lake District, towards Manchester. The dry ground on top of it has developed a fine show of heather. Descend gently to canal bridge No.87 and cross and turn right to rejoin the towpath. The former filter beds of the paper works down on your left have now become a nature reserve under the auspices of the County Council and Lancashire Trust for Nature Conservation. As well as open water, there are reedbeds, marsh, and scrub in which a variety of plants and birds may be seen. A gate by the bridge from which you started gives access to boardwalks and a bird hide and a nearby notice gives a map of the reserve and explains how to contact the warden. Complete the circuit by going back over the bridge.

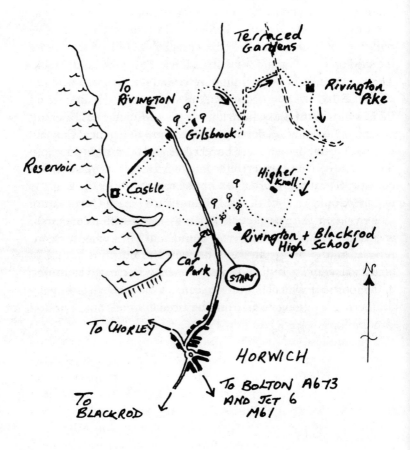

Terraced Gardens

To Rivington

Gilsbrook

Rivington Pike

Reservoir

Castle

Higher knoll

Rivington + Blackrod High School

Car Park

START

N

To CHORLEY

HORWICH

To BOLTON A673 AND JCT 6 M61

To BLACKROD

# RIVINGTON

## WALK 25

### 3 miles (5 km)

### OS Landranger 109

Across to the right of the route north into Lancashire, whether you take the M6 or the old A6, the separate hill of Rivington Pike stands out boldly from the slopes of Winter Hill behind it. It was, no doubt, the view westward from here that persuaded Lord Leverhulme (who was born in nearby Bolton) to purchase the Rivington estate in 1899 and to indulge his passion for landscape design. This lasted until he died, in 1925, and the whole was left to slow dereliction until Liverpool Corporation took over in 1947. After some basic tidying operations the estate was again left to its own devices until about 1974 when a major programme of re-instatement began. The outcome is public access to a very interesting combination of man-created landscape and moorland which is quite unique. This walk explores the southern end of Lever Park, the Terraced Gardens above it, and circuits back over Rivington Pike.

The simplest approach is from the northern end of Horwich where you should take Lever Park Avenue from just beyond the large roundabout on the A673. In about ¾ mile, park on the left a little past Rivington and Blackrod High School on the right (GR: SD 635128). An information centre, restaurant and toilets are to be found in a further ¾ mile at Great House Barn – this is, of itself, interesting as a fine example of a cruckbuilt tithe barn.

Walk out of the car park through birch and oak scrub at the bottom end and join an avenue lined with sycamores. Turn left and walk down to the reconstruction of the ruin of Liverpool

Castle on the shore of Rivington Lower reservoir (the original castle stood in Liverpool where Derby Square is now). It is possible, and worthwhile, to work your way round the outside of the walls and to squint a view into the inside. Unfortunately, vandalism prevents open access without considerable (no doubt costly) work on the structure. Having made the circuit, walk towards the Pike along the centre of the three tracks which join the semi-circular track before the castle. Pass a stone and brown-painted house to the left to reach Rivington Lane and cross to a track in a clough enclosed with hollies and yews.

The track leads up past a private house called 'Gilsbrook' on your right. Continue ahead at the top of the garden railings. The track curves round to the left. Turn right on a track uphill, marked with a yellow arrow, beside a stream and enter a gate at the bottom of the Terraced Gardens at the Ravine. Bear up steeply to the right, outside the trees, to reach a further track coming up from your right and turn hard left to enter the gardens again through a gate. The view opens to the west from Fiddler's Ferry power station in the Mersey valley round through Ashurst Beacon, to Chorley and Southport on the coast. Immediately to your right inside the gate is a set of steps. Turn up them and you have now joined the route of a detailed garden trail at post No.8 and shortly enter the Japanese Garden with its lake which was designed by the Windermere-based gardener T H Mawson in 1922. Points 10 and 11 indicate the places in which tea houses once stood. Much of the garden area has suffered greatly from the overgrowth of rhododendrons but there are still many other interesting species to be found along the trail. At the far side of the lake bear to the right past Point 13, where the gardeners' work sheds used to be, and go up the steps past the red-topped post to reach George's Lane just south of a toilet block. A few hundred yards further on is the other tower of Rivington, The Dovecot or Pigeon Tower, built by Lord Leverhulme. As an alternative, this can also be reached by following the trail to post No.29 and you can then return along George's Lane.

Almost opposite the toilet block a path leads up to Rivington Pike itself. At 1,198 feet this has always formed an ideal site for a warning beacon and it was certainly used at the time of the Spanish Armada in 1588. The tower which stands on the top was built in 1733 and originally had access but vandalism, sadly, made it necessary to block up the entrances when it was restored. The claim is that the view – on exceptionally fine, clear days – extends as far as Anglesey (80 miles away) and the top of Bowfell, in the Lake District. Certainly, you will want to linger and see what you can identify though it's worth remembering that Winter Hill, behind you, is well named and it can be extremely cold up here.

Drop down from the tower and edge right to rejoin George's Lane once more about ½ mile below where you left it. Immediately across is a stile by a gate which leads to a track which goes down past Higher Knoll and then swings round by a small quarry to a junction of tracks behind the High School. Turn right along the school fence and then drop left through the wood on any of many paths to pass by the playing fields to reach the road across from the car park from which you started.

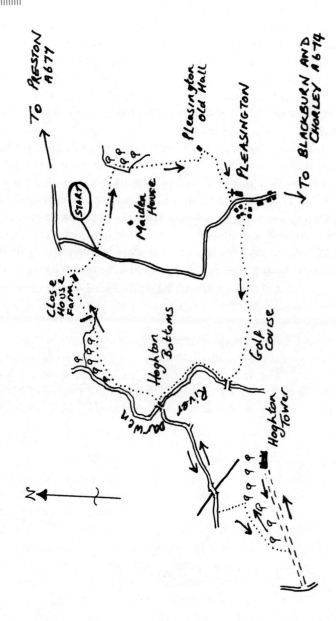

# PLEASINGTON

In the angle between the old (A674) and new (A677) – well 'new' in about 1820 – main roads between Blackburn and Preston lies an area of countryside, either side of the valley of the river Darwen, which remains surprisingly secretive despite its closeness to urban central Lancashire. This is country with great attractiveness and not a little history but without the dominance and pushiness of the higher hills. Its quiet corners are a retreat for a surprising amount of wildlife and are well worth the minor effort to discover. The walk described lies entirely on the eastern bank of the river with a possible spur to include a visit to Hoghton Tower.

Take the lane to Pleasington either from the A674 at Livesey, on the western edge of Blackburn, or off the A677, south, at the top of the hill at Beardwood on the Preston road into Blackburn. Park by the roadside close to the entrance of Maiden House Farm a little north of the village (GR: SD 638277).

Start by walking 50 yards up the entrance track of Maiden House Farm (there is no footpath sign) and go ahead along the field edge beside a row of oak trees continuing straight ahead to dip down a little and then rise to the corner of a wood below a house to the left. Across to the right there is a wide view of the West Pennine Moors from Darwen Tower, through Great Hill to Winter Hill. Ten yards inside the wood turn right down a slope to follow a clear path by a broken wall and the former workings of Butler's Delf. At the bottom of the wood aim just left of the three isolated trees in the middle of the large field to a stile in the bottom right hand corner in a copse of beech trees. To your left is Pleasington Old Hall, dated 1587.

Turn right past some renovated buildings and follow the lane through to the road in the village. Immediately to your left is the RC church of St Mary and St John the Baptist. Built in 1819, it is remarkable for its style and large size and has recently undergone extensive refurbishment. Cross over the road and go left to Priory Close, beside the Butler's Arms – John Francis Butler built the church. At the back-left of the cul-de-sac a footpath leads down to the fields through bracken and Himalayan balsam. Take the old track line, with a hedge to your left, looking down into the valley of the Trout brook on the right where a large and obvious conduit crosses on narrow pillars. Directly ahead is the rocky bluff on top of which Hoghton Tower stands hidden by trees. Halfway down, at the foot of the cliff, is the Blackburn to Preston railway line. As you descend to the valley of the Darwen the path skirts a golf course and the vegetation changes to heather and fine grasses, the former producing a fine display in August. The wall has a number of elder trees along it with their early season edible flowers and later, equally edible berries. Ahead is the hamlet at the Victoria Road end of Hoghton Bottoms. The path reaches a stone bridge over the river with a stile on the right just before it.

Walk downstream along the river bank. For many years the Darwen was one of the most polluted rivers in the county and still suffers from an excess of plastic litter which catches in the overhanging branches during winter floods. Here, however, you may be lucky, as I have been, to see the metallic-blue flash of a kingfisher as it moves between fishing perches. This, at least, suggests things are improving a good deal and the water now runs much clearer than it used to. Along this section, also, you will pass a rabbit warren on your right. The path reaches Hoghton Bottoms at a green iron footbridge at Valley Road.

If you wish to make the diversion, and return, to Hoghton Tower, cross over the bridge and walk up the road to cross the railway bridge. A little beyond, on the left, is a signed path which leads up to the edge of the woods. Turn right and work your way round to meet the driveway up to the tower. Entrance to Hoghton Tower is only available on summer Sundays and you need to time your arrival carefully (Tel: 0254 852986). The de Hoghtons have been in this area since the time of the Norman invasion. The tower was, however, not begun until the 1560s and took perhaps 150 years to reach its present general shape. It was extensively restored in the nineteenth century. Perhaps its greatest claim to fame is the story that James I 'knighted' a particularly flavoursome loin of beef – hence 'sirloin' – during his visit in 1617.

Back at the bridge, continue downriver by walking through the garden of Lower Park Farm and follow the arrows left round the end of the building. Just beyond a wooden Scout Hut on your right an obvious track begins to rise up the bank along the edge of woods and the slope to the left quickly turns into a narrow gorge-like valley with magnificent foliage colours in autumn. Almost at the top of the bank the track bends round left as it crosses a shallow side valley. At this point make to the right up the valley and reach a stile in a wall on the left. Walk up the field to the buildings of Close House Farm. At the cattle grid at the far end, beyond the house, turn right over the stile and walk round the garden to go through a fence and hedge line and bear left along it to pass a small reservoir surrounded by a round wall. Walk ahead to the field gate at the road close to the start point.

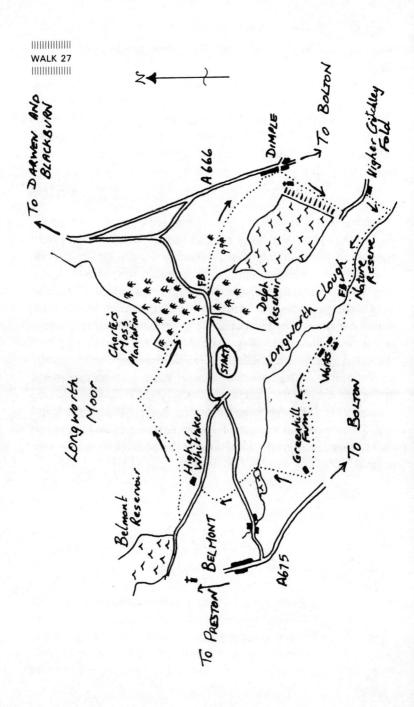

N

TO DARWEN AND BLACKBURN

TO BOLTON

DIMPLE

A 666

Higher Griley Fold

FB

9 PH

FB

Charters Moss Plantation

Delph Reservoir

Longworth Clough

START

Longworth Moor

Nature Reserve

High Whittaker

Works

FB

Greenhill Farm

Belmont Reservoir

TO BOLTON

A 675

BELMONT

TO PRESTON

# LONGWORTH VALLEY

WALK 27

5 miles (8 km)

OS Landranger 109

The upper part of the valley of the Longworth brook lies within the county as a small enclave chopped off by the boundary with Bolton. The best known place – the only place – within it is the village of Belmont which stands four-square, as it were, at the moorland edge, the spire of St Peter's being visible from almost everywhere around. The route of the walk links the valley bottom and the grazed moor together with the plantations which surround the tributary Delph brook.

The start is at the corner of Charter's Moss plantation where the lanes meet in a T junction and there is ample roadside parking (GR: SD 693162). Approach either from the A675, at the lower end of Belmont and through Belmont Works and straight across the crossroads at the top of the hill, or use the A666 to the Darwen side of Dimple and bear first left.

Walk first towards the A666 to the bend and take the gate just beyond the plantation edge on the right. The path drops to a footbridge over the stream feeding Delph reservoir. Up the bank across the field you enter a larch plantation with sycamore, rowan, hawthorn and alder scattered along the path side with sitka spruce and Scots pine at the far end. The boats of the Delph Sailing Club will be in view once you leave the trees and the long skyline of Smithills Moor and Winter Hill dominate the west, Turton Heights complementing them up to your left. The path becomes a track now and heads for the hamlet of Dimple with the Thomas Dutton restaurant on the main road. As you enter the street (one side of which has now been demolished) you cross the county boundary.

At the archway behind the Thomas Dutton, turn right to go down hill between two pillars and walk along the boundary wall to Walmsley Unitarian chapel with the school beside it. The former was founded pre-1672 and this building is of 1713. The school is dated 1851 and remained in use until around 1980. Pass in front of them and down between the walls to a bridge over the brook at the bottom and re-enter Lancashire. The dam covers the site of the former Delph Mill which was, at one time, part-owned by Samuel Crompton, inventor of the mule for cotton spinning. In about 1813 the mill-pond burst its banks and swept the mill away. Continue gently up to the road and turn left. The view south, from here, includes most of Greater Manchester.

A short distance along the road, at the bend, cross over to enter a gate on the right just before the buildings of Higher Critchley Fold (there is no footpath sign) and walk down the bank into Longworth Clough with Dunscar golf course occupying the slope opposite. Bear right along the track in the bottom of the clough with the chimneys of Springside Paper Works clearly ahead. Pass a small red-brick building by the river and then a concrete electricity building. The section from here to the works is a Lancashire Trust for Nature Conservation reserve which is famous for its wealth of flowers in the marshy valley bottom. Small carrs of alder and willow are scattered along the way and rowan and hawthorn bloom profusely. Mayflowers, bistort and marsh marigold are to be found and meadowsweet grows in tall drifts of creamy-white flowers. A clear path crosses the river and passes a reserve sign as you enter the works.

Continue on as near a straight line as you are able, first up some shallow steps, and then a ramp, and bear right between the paper stacks and past the open wash tanks to keep right and drop slightly back across the valley beside some large circular holding tanks. A track bears off to the left to reach Lower Fold Farm in 200 yards. Take the surfaced track to the left across fields with tumbledown walls to the buildings of Greenhill Farm a little short of the main road. Just beyond the garden there is a stile to the right. (The Wright's Arms is available for refreshment just 100 yards to the right along the road.) Leave the side clough to your right and zig-zag to the valley bottom beside the sluice in the dam of Belmont Lodge. The view up towards the church is especially attractive from here. The route crosses the dam and then climbs sharply up to the road where there is a limited amount of alternative parking.

Turn left and then cross to the right through the second of two gates and go up between an old wall and a wire fence. Leave the buildings of Lower Whittaker to the left and swing up along the wall to join a lane opposite Higher Whittaker. Walk left along the lane towards the dam of Belmont reservoir (also with its sailing club). This gives a good view of most of Belmont. Much of the village is the original stone but there are a few modern additions which have rather spoilt the whole, mainly because the lie of the roof-lines is out of keeping. At the corner of the small wood just before the reservoir turn over the stile on the right and bear hard back, passing just right of a wooden fence round a water tank in the field to find a gate at the angle of the wall behind Higher Whittaker. The view down-valley over Manchester is even wider now than before and the great flank of Longworth Moor rises up to your left. Follow the wall on your left along two fields to a gate and stile at the corner of a new plantation. The path bears slightly left along the line of a drainage ditch to drop across a small clough and reach a track 100 yards beyond. Turn right along this and go through an area of diggings, walking beside the edge of Charter's Moss plantation to reach the start point once again.

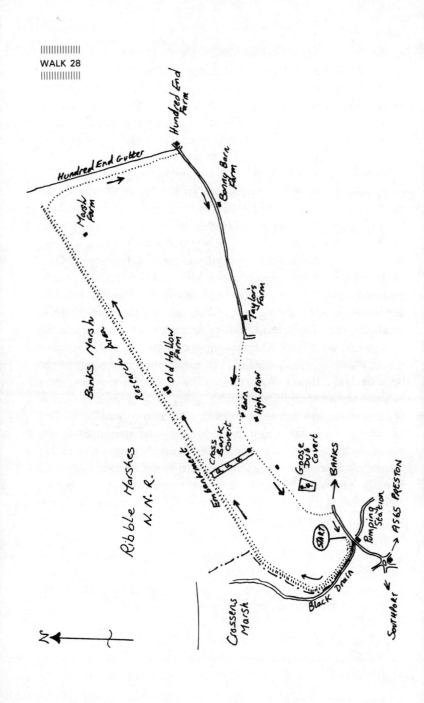

# BANKS AND RIBBLE MARSHES

## WALK 28

★

7½ miles (12 km)

OS Landranger 102

Although the boundary changes of 1974 withdrew the coast south of the Ribble estuary from Lancashire the estuary itself and, consequently, almost all the Ribble Marshes National Nature Reserve and the adjacent Ribble Estuary Site of Special Scientific Interest remained within the county. This walk is along the coast beside them and takes you away from the more easily accessible, and therefore more crowded, north Southport shore. The reason for both the NNR and the SSSI is the massive wintering flocks of wildfowl and waders on the estuary which are impressive, even if you are not particularly interested in birdlife. At all times of the year there is a bracing breeze to fill the lungs and wide horizons across the saltmarshes, the mudflats, and out to sea and good views of the inland hills. If you do want to watch the birds then a check with the tide tables (available from: James Laver Printing Co Ltd, Argyle Street, Liverpool 1) is worthwhile. The best months for birds are September and October, the worst June and July, and the best time to start off is about ½ hour before high tide. By this time the rising water will have driven the feeding flocks eastwards on to Crossens Marsh seaward from the embankment. Later they will be pushed off this too and many will move back to the marshy fields inland of the sandworks on the Marine Drive route in to Southport.

Approach the start from the A565 Preston road at the roundabout by The Plough at Crossens at the northern end of Southport. Refreshment is available here and 1½ miles into town will give you a choice of everything from fish and chips to 5 star hotel. Southport is the only resort I have ever come across where you can eat and drink at midnight on any day of the year (at least, all those I've tried – and that's most!). Turn for Banks and park on the left in about 500 yards opposite Crossens pumping station (GR: SD 377207). All the mosslands on the landward side of Southport are drained by continuous pumping. Now the pumps are electrically run the numbers of stations have been reduced and the Black Drain and its adjacent sluice are the main northern outlet for the water.

Go through beside the gate which carries the notice 'Keep out dangerous water' and on to the public path along the top of the embankment on the Banks side of the Black Drain, the near edge of which is the County boundary. Very shortly you will come to a Ribble Marshes NNR map and sign which tells you that shooting for wildfowl takes place between 1 September and 20 February annually. Immediately over the Drain is the Southport sewage works and the Marine Drive. The latter is built on the bed of the old railway to Preston and the weakness of the sand below causes continual problems with subsidence, cars often being seen to bounce their way along it.

The view north west is dominated by Blackpool Tower. As the crow flies it is barely 6 miles away but the lowest crossing of the river remains at Preston so it is 30 miles by road. Rather more directly across is the white-painted windmill on the foreshore at Lytham St Annes. Immediately at your feet stretches a vast area of saltmarsh with its unique collection of plants which can withstand the twice-daily inundation by the tide. Islands of green are intercut with gutters and runnels which drain and fill with each tide and provide feeding grounds for a variety of birds at all times of the year. Oystercatcher and shelduck breed here and curlew, lapwing and dunlin are seen in numbers.

The autumn flocks also include redshank, knot, sanderling, bar-tailed godwit, grey plover, and ringed plover. Less frequent are little stint, greenshank, spotted redshank, and

114

black-tailed godwit. Common, arctic, and Sandwich terns can be seen and, more rarely, roseate and little terns too. All these birds attract, of course, those who feed on them and sparrowhawk, short-eared owl, hen harrier, peregrine, and merlin all take rich pickings from time to time. Flocks of thousands of pink-footed geese feed here in autumn and winter as do large congregations of swans – especially whooper and Bewick's. Wigeon and shoveler ducks are joined, on occasion, by rarities like scoter.

The walk continues easily along the embankment past Cross Bank covert, a shelterbelt of trees, and Old Hollow and Marsh farms until there is no choice but to turn back inland up Hundred End Gutter to the far entrance to the reserve across the road from Hundred End Farm and beside a modern Georgian-style property. On the way you will pass several more NNR notices and a series of small, automatic sluices. These switch on with a considerable roar and make you jump if they catch you unawares. For a while, near Old Hollow, part of Banks Marsh is a sanctuary reserved for research purposes. As you walk along the Bowland fells stand out half left and Winter Hill, behind Bolton, is half right. These embankments are part of a series which began in the middle of the 19th century at Hesketh marsh, a little further up the Ribble, and continued well into this century. The object was mainly to clear the channel for shipping into the port at Preston but it also, of course, resulted in the reclamation of some rich arable land which grows magnificent crops of vegetables like carrots and cauliflowers. Many of the farms associate this with crops under glass as well.

Turn right along Marsh Road where care is needed for the first few hundred yards until the footway starts beyond Bonny Barn Farm. In about ½ mile the lane right-angles to the left just after Taylor's Farm. Walk ahead here into the field and follow the bank on the left to pass a barn and High Brow 200 yards to the left. Continue as nearly straight on as is possible to reach an abandoned house at the inland end of Cross Bank covert and follow the green, grassy lane on its left and stay with the footpath signs to bend left down a track to pass Goose Dub covert on your left and to exit beside the end of a row of houses some 200 yards from the start.

# RUFFORD, MERE SANDS WOOD, AND MARTIN MERE

WALK 29

8¾ miles (14 km)

OS Landranger 108

Should you choose to drive to Martin Mere, rather than walk the spur route to it, this walk is reduced to no more than 5, very easy, miles. There are shops and pubs in Rufford village, and cafés at both Rufford Old Hall and at Martin Mere, and excellent picnic facilities at Mere Sands Wood. I suggest that you start from Mere Sands Wood but you could, equally well, park by the road near St Mary's church in Rufford or, indeed, at Martin Mere: your choice will depend on where you place priorities.

Despite the parallel M6, the A59 between Liverpool and Preston still carries a heavy flow of traffic and it is most unexpected that this small village, which it cuts in half, is a focus for three of the most interesting venues in the North. The black and white, half-timbered, Rufford Old Hall is a National Trust property and is open between April and the end of October, except for Fridays, the Hall itself opening between 1 pm and 5 pm. Mere Sands Wood is a Lancashire Trust for Conservation reserve (there is a small parking fee – NB members only on Sundays) developed from former sand pits. Martin Mere belongs to the Wildfowl and Wetlands Trust and has a collection of birds which rivals their headquarters at Slimbridge. These latter two are open all year. Visiting all three will take a full day.

The start is most easily reached by taking the B5246 road (signed Holmeswood and Southport) from the Hesketh Arms and turn left after about a mile on a track to the car park and toilets at Mere Sands Wood where, at the edge of the car park,

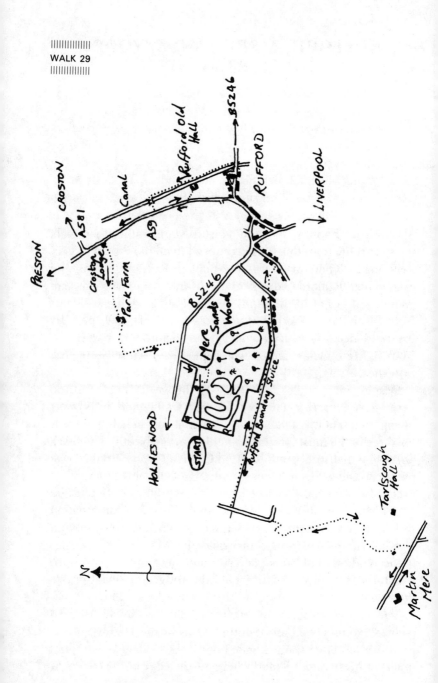

the Lancashire Trust operates an information kiosk (GR: SD 464156). Various trails are signed within the reserve and a descriptive leaflet is available. There are several public viewing hides, one of which is suitable for the disabled.

The reserve is classified as a Site of Special Scientific Interest for the exposures of the Shirdley Hill sand, the coarse, rounded grains of which indicate that it was deposited as dunes after the end of the last Ice Age, perhaps 10,000 years ago. It is the digging of this sand which left behind the lakes and small ponds within the wood of oak, birch and Scots pine that give such variety to the reserve. Between the lakes are areas of heathland marsh. The bird list is extensive. In addition to spring and autumn migrants you should find coot, moorhen, teal, mallard and dabchick, pheasant, woodpigeon, blackbird, robin and mistle thrush at almost any time. The waterfowl list includes, at least, goldeneye, tufted duck, pochard, ruddy duck, gadwall and goosander. Consult the wardens for an up-to-date list of sightings. The woodland, itself, has the odd tree of special interest, Turkey oak, for instance, and fungi are abundant in a damp autumn. Red squirrels are regularly seen and the wood is visited by foxes.

The trails of Mere Sands Wood may be taken in any order and at any pace. When you decide to move on make for the southern edge of the wood beside the deep ditch of the Rufford Boundary Sluice. If you plan to walk through to Martin Mere, turn west along the sluice to the lane (Sandyway) and then walk left to the right-angled bend. A footpath leads off by the old hedge to cross over a ditch on a footbridge and is signed right and then left along fences to cross fields towards the buildings of Tarlscough Hall which you can see to the south. Before reaching the farm bear right on a track and past a tumbledown cottage to join a lane. Five hundred yards to the right will bring you to Martin Mere.

To try to describe the marvellous visitor facilities, wildfowl collection and other bird visitors and residents at Martin Mere in a short space is quite impracticable. The entrance fee is well worth it. Most of the pathways and hides are accessible by wheelchair and, unusually, there is a trail for the visually handicapped. It is open every day, except Christmas and Boxing Days. The Wildfowl and Wetland Trust has developed the Martin Mere site since the early 1970s. This was the last area of undrained peat mossland in Lancashire and was slowly drying out and becoming covered in vegetation. The water is now maintained at a high level by pumping and the open water has been extended considerably. Some 120 species of waterfowl from all over the world are kept in the 45 acre waterfowl gardens, the 550-odd acres of the remainder attracting vast numbers of migrant birds – 16,000 or more pink-footed geese alone in autumn and winter. It is easy to see why this is a wetland reserve with international status! Greylag, Canada, barnacle, bean, and white-fronted geese are all regularly to be seen and, more rarely, a snowgoose passes through. All three swans are here – mute, Bewick's and whooper – and most of our wild ducks. Waders abound on the muddy water margins: snipe, oystercatcher, ruff, golden plover and many more. The drainage ditches support a great range of other species, including some gorgeously coloured dragonflies!

Eventually you will want to reverse your route to Mere Sands Wood and walk through along the sluice behind the houses and cross the lane past the cricket ground to turn left and walk to the village centre across the A59. Walk up by St Mary's church to the canal bridge and join the towpath on the far bank and walk north. Across the canal is Rufford Old Hall surrounded by gardens. You have to pass by to cross on a wooden swing-bridge and rejoin the footway on the main road to backtrack slightly to the entrance to the hall.

In a walk of superlatives, Rufford Old Hall is another outstanding experience. The core of it is 15th century with a brick wing of 1662 and a linking section of 1821. It belonged originally to the Hesketh family (who moved, eventually, to the new hall across the A59). The black and white timbers and the infill with quatrefoil designs make a delightful picture in the garden setting. Inside is a massive hammer-beam roof with much carving, and a unique medieval carved oak screen – theoretically movable if you can raise the manpower to achieve it. There are collections of arms and armour, 17th century furniture, a priests' hole, and a Beauvais tapestry, amongst other treasures. Several rooms contain items illustrating particular themes: a village kitchen, dresses, dolls, and pottery.

Return from the Hall by walking along the main road towards Preston as far as the bridleway sign beside Croston Lodge Stables and walk west up the track through Park Farm. Turn first left to rejoin Holmeswood Road only a little distance from the entrance to Mere Sands Wood car park.

APPLEY BRIDGE

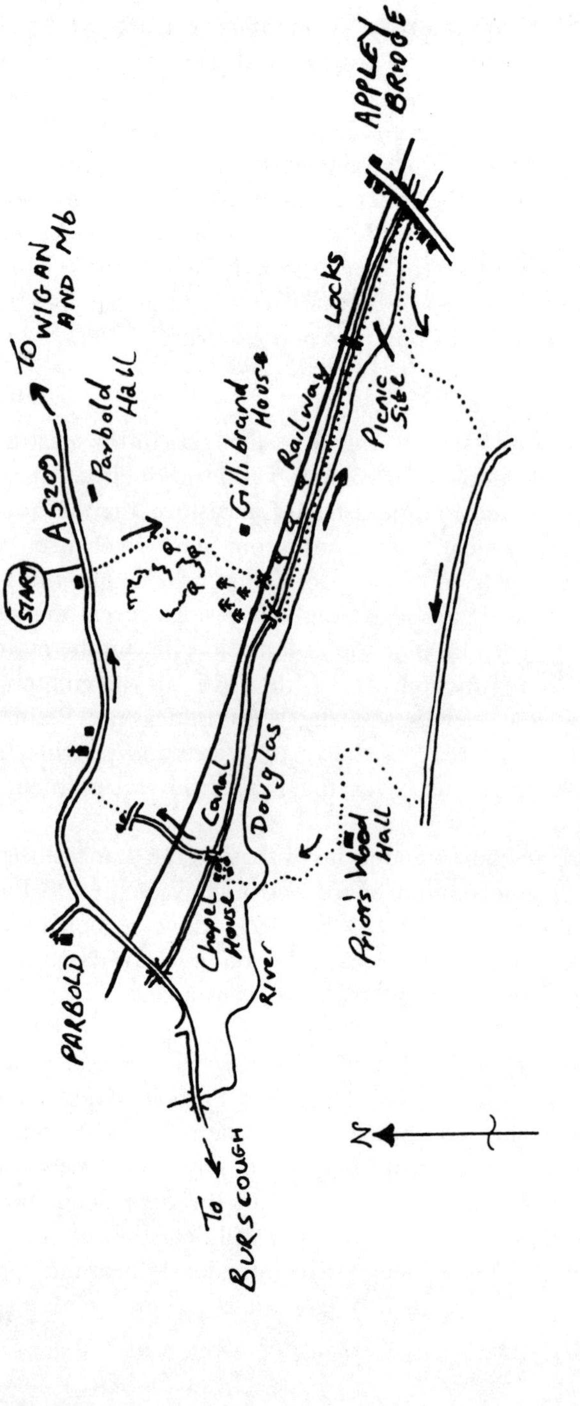

TO WIGAN AND M6

Parbold Hall

A5209

START

Gillibrand House

Railway

Locks

Picnic Site

Parbold Hall

Canal

Douglas

Chapel House

River

Priors Wood Hall

PARBOLD

TO BURSCOUGH

N

# PARBOLD HILL AND THE DOUGLAS VALLEY

WALK 30

★

4¾ miles (7.5 km)

OS Landranger 108

The narrow valley of the river Douglas to the west of Wigan marks the sudden transition to rural tranquillity from the great swathe of the old industrial Lancashire that is now in the Greater Manchester conurbation. The river itself and the parallel Leeds and Liverpool Canal have strong links with an industrial past and even the valley sides reveal their scars on closer inspection. The top of Parbold Hill, on the main A5209 link from Junction 27 of the M6 at Shevington, has a magnificent view across the West Lancashire Plain and the mouth of the Mersey to North Wales and provides a handy starting point just over the road from refreshment at The Wiggin Tree.

Park in the extended layby beside the Lancashire County Council information board and a copy of the OS Pathfinder footpath map (GR: SD 508107). Have a look at the view indicator before you leave – on a clear day the Berwyn Mountains are visible over 40 miles away.

Follow the footpath sign down towards the valley on a well-surfaced path past the abandoned Parbold sandstone quarries on the right. To your left is the rather fine Georgian pile of Parbold Hall. Part of the quarries have been used as a waste-disposal site and as you descend through woodland of oak, birch, beech and sycamore you will hear the roar of gas being burnt off. This seems to disturb the local pheasants, partridge, and flocks of blue and great tits not a whit. Cross the entrance track into the tip and go down past Gillibrand House on the left. The small plantations of Norway spruce and Scots pine around the railway line are on the spoil heaps of the former Gillibrand coal mine. Once across the railway bear right and down to the stone-arched bridge (No.40) over the canal and join the towpath to the left.

The full 58 miles of the canal took 46 years to build, starting in 1770. The adjacent river Douglas hardly seems like its predecessor to look at it today but it carried coal on the small barges known as Mersey flats, using 18 locks, between Wigan and the Ribble estuary at Tarleton between 1742 and 1774 when this section of the canal opened, and regular cargo traffic on the canal ended only in 1972. Sadly, the waters of the Douglas still carry obvious pollution and the canal always appears a good deal clearer and cleaner, especially on a crisp winter's day. Spring and summer see great bird activity with nesting mallard, moorhen and coot and plenty of the common birds of woodland and hedgerow across the canal and beside the sheep-grazed fields. Bridge 41 shows the grooves worn into the sandstone by the ropes by which horses used to tow the barges along. Just beyond are Appley locks – the first since Liverpool – with a single 12 foot lock nearest to you and two smaller ones added later to speed up traffic. On the far bank, between this point and the modern concrete bridge at Appley Lane is a large building material works. This stretch is popular with fishermen who sit in apparently dour enjoyment with their backs to the recently created picnic site on the southern bank. There is alternative parking here by the canal and refreshment at the Railway and the Inn Between.

At the bridge turn away from the canal, crossing the river bridge (rebuilt in 1903), and go immediately to the right before the first cottage along the river bank to head down the valley – there is no footpath sign. Directly across in a garden is the statue of a young girl which looks as though she originally held a globe in her hands. Follow the bank past a weir and a massive pipe crossing the river to a broken stile where a yellow arrow points the right of way across the field (not round it) to a footbridge at the far hedge. Follow left up the stream through scrub woodland along a rather muddy stretch of path to reach a lane just right of Lees trout lake.

Turn right and pass Martins Farm. Parbold Hall and Christ church, on the hill, stand out on the skyline. Fields on both right and left of the lane are reclaimed from former tips. It is sheltered along here and I have found white deadnettle in flower in January. The chimney of an old brickworks will come into view ahead on the left but before you reach this turn right along a track by the wall of the garden of the second farm house on the right – again there is no footpath sign. The track bends to the right a little and then drops towards the valley down a small wooded clough in which there is a shoot marked out. Beyond, swing left across the cattle grid and up past a copse on your right to skirt a new plantation of larch and reach the rear of the large farm of Priors Wood Hall. The spire of the other (RC) church in Parbold village will be in sight ahead: one of the oldest Christian sites in the county. Walk towards it between the farmyard and the new slurry tank and down the field to the left of an oak tree to cross a bridge and go through the gates on the far side. Turn right now past a massive concrete cover of the main pipe to Hoscar sewage works as far as a wood and iron footbridge taking you back across the river Douglas with a very poor stile at the far end. Aim up the field towards the left of the cottages at Chapel House. You will emerge on a lane beside a cross recording the site of a 16th century chapel.

Cross the fold between the cottages and walk up over the canal bridge along the lane to the level crossing. Carefully cross the railway and walk up the hill to the T junction. Almost immediately over the lane is a stile (with no sign) beside a garden hedge. Enter the field and walk up the left hand boundary to the main road opposite Lindsay House Rest Home and use the footway to the right to Christ church. This is the church which replaced the chapel in the valley below. Return up the footway to the start past the old school, now a private nursery school.

125